THE PROFESSIONAL ETHICS
TOOLKIT

CHRISTOPHER MEYERS

THE PROFESSIONAL ETHICS
TOOLKIT

WILEY Blackwell

The right of Christopher Meyers to be identified as the author of this work has been asserted in accordance with law.

Registered Office
John Wiley & Sons, Inc., 111 River Street, Hoboken, NJ 07030, USA
John Wiley & Sons Ltd, The Atrium, Southern Gate, Chichester, West Sussex, PO19 8SQ, UK

Editorial Office
9600 Garsington Road, Oxford, OX4 2DQ, UK

For details of our global editorial offices, customer services, and more information about Wiley products visit us at www.wiley.com.

Wiley also publishes its books in a variety of electronic formats and by print-on-demand. Some content that appears in standard print versions of this book may not be available in other formats.

Library of Congress Cataloging-in-Publication Data

Names: Meyers, Christopher, 1957– author.
Title: The professional ethics toolkit / by Christopher Meyers.
Description: First edition. | Hoboken, NJ, USA : John Wiley & Sons Ltd, 2018. |
    Includes bibliographical references and index.
Identifiers: LCCN 2017047294 (print) | LCCN 2017052284 (ebook) | ISBN 9781119045175 (pdf) |
    ISBN 9781119045182 (epub) | ISBN 9781119045168 (cloth) | ISBN 9781119045151 (pbk.)
Subjects: LCSH: Professional ethics.
Classification: LCC BJ1725 (ebook) | LCC BJ1725 .M49 2018 (print) | DDC 174–dc23
LC record available at https://lccn.loc.gov/2017047294

Cover Images: (Background) © Tashatuvango/Shutterstock; (Microchip) © Iaroslav Neliubov/Shutterstock; (Veterinarian) © Zivica Kerkez/Shutterstock; (Doctors) © Olena Yakobchuk/Shutterstock; (Professor) © sirtravelalot/Shutterstock; (Gavel and scale) © one photo/Shutterstock; (Workers) © Christian Lagerek/Shutterstock; (Toolkit images) © Winston Link/Shutterstock; © pictafolio/Gettyimages; © ProstoVova/Gettyimages; © Science Photo Library/Shutterstock; © Thomas Northcut/Gettyimages; © Keith Bell/Shutterstock; © jgroup/Gettyimages
Cover Design: Wiley

Set in 10.5/13pt Minion by SPi Global, Pondicherry, India

Printed in the UK by Bell & Bain Ltd, Glasgow

10 9 8 7 6 5 4 3 2 1

To my family, in gratitude for the inspiration and joy you provide every single day.

Contents

Acknowledgments   xii

Introduction   **1**

Opening Thoughts   2
Being and Acting Professional   5
Definition and Listing   6
Cases   7
    Health-care professionals and the conscience clause   7
    Defending the indefensible   8
    Getting by with cheaper materials   9
Note   10
References   10

Part I   Theory, Concepts, and Ethics Reasoning   **11**

1 Historical Overview and Definitional Questions   **13**

  1.1 Some History   16
      1.1.1 The rising role of science   17
      1.1.2 Impact of the European Enlightenment   18
      1.1.3 Organizing to differentiate   19
      1.1.4 Formalizing the standards   20
      1.1.5 Establishing trust   21
      1.1.6 Monopolies, money, and power   22

1.2	Defining "Professional"	23
	1.2.1 Essential features	24
	1.2.2 Common features	26
	1.2.3 Role-based duties	28
1.3	A Working List	30
1.4	Types of Professional–Client Relationships	32
	1.4.1 Agency	33
	1.4.2 Paternalistic (or parentalistic)	33
	1.4.3 Contractual	34
	1.4.4 Affinity	34
	1.4.5 Fiduciary	35
	Notes	35
	References	36

2 A Model of Ethics Reasoning — **38**

2.1	Relativism, Absolutism, and Contextualism	40
2.2	Deontology	43
	2.2.1 Immanuel Kant	44
2.3	Utilitarianism	48
	2.3.1 John Stuart Mill	49
2.4	Context, Context, Context	51
2.5	Ross and Pluralistic Deontology	53
2.6	A Model of Ethics Reasoning	57
	2.6.1 A method and steps	59
2.7	Moral Principles	63
2.8	Case: Cutting Corners	65
	Notes	66
	References	66

Part II   Concepts, Principles, and Norms within Professional Environments — **69**

3 Autonomy and Respect for Persons — **73**

3.1	Autonomy in the World	75
	3.1.1 Kant and moral agency	77
	3.1.2 Mill and developed selfhood	79
	3.1.3 Variable autonomy, life plans, and identity	80
	3.1.4 Contributing and detracting factors	81

3.2   The Hard Work of Being Autonomous   82
      3.2.1 Additional examples   84
3.3   Case: Which Autonomous Voice?   86
      Notes   88
      References   88

4 Beneficence and Non-Maleficence   90

4.1   Beneficence   93
      4.1.1 Finding balance in the professions   94
      4.1.2 Paternalistic beneficence?   95
4.2   Non-Maleficence   97
      4.2.1 Harm and incompetence   98
4.3   Cases   100
      4.3.1 Mandatory vaccinations?   100
      4.3.2 How much should you give?   101
      Notes   102
      References   103

5 Competency   105

5.1   Systematizing Confidence   106
5.2   Case: Sanctioning a Colleague   111
      Note   112

6 Confidentiality and Privacy   113

6.1   Privacy   115
6.2   Privacy as a Moral Root of Confidentiality   116
      6.2.1 Intimacy and confidentiality   117
      6.2.2 Deontological and utilitarian foundations   118
6.3   Practical Considerations   120
      6.3.1 Weighing confidentiality against other principles 121
6.4   Cases   122
      6.4.1 Balancing principles: Privacy, beneficence,
             non-maleficence, honesty, and fidelity   122
      6.4.2 Tell the family?   123
      Notes   124
      References   125

7 Conflict of Interest   **126**

   7.1 Definition   128
      7.1.1 Situational conflict of interest   129
      7.1.2 Conflict of interest and individual choices   130
      7.1.3 Psychology and character   131
   7.2 Types of Conflicting Inducements   132
      7.2.1 Material inducements   132
      7.2.2 Perceived conflict of interest   133
      7.2.3 Conflicts of obligation and bias   134
   7.3 Structural Conflict of Interest   136
      7.3.1 Universally present   137
      7.3.2 Roles and conflict of interest   137
      7.3.3 Bias and conflict of interest   138
      7.3.4 Managing structural conflict of interest   138
   7.4 Cases   140
      7.4.1 Accepting a gift   140
      7.4.2 What now?   141
      7.4.3 Treating everyone equally   142
      Notes   143
      References   144

8 Fidelity, Honesty, and Role-Based Duties   **146**

   8.1 Promises   148
      8.1.1 Moral foundations   149
   8.2 Honesty   150
      8.2.1 Professionals' duty to be informed   151
      8.2.2 Commission versus omission   152
      8.2.3 Honesty and wisdom   153
      8.2.4 Balancing duties   154
      8.2.5 Honesty and roles   155
   8.3 Cases   156
      8.3.1 Committed to the company?   156
      8.3.2 A contract is a contract   158
      8.3.3 The lying ethicist   159
      Notes   160
      References   161

9 Formal Justice, Bias, and Allocation of Resources   **162**

  9.1   Arbitrary Features   163
  9.2   The Complexity of Justice   165
  9.3   Formal Justice   166
     9.3.1   Justice and objectivity   167
     9.3.2   Negative impacts   168
     9.3.3   Circumstantial responses   168
  9.4   Bias   170
     9.4.1   Managing bias   171
  9.5   Distributive Justice   172
     9.5.1   What is fair?   173
     9.5.2   Rawls's theory   174
  9.6   Cases   176
     9.6.1   Equal treatment for cheaters?   176
     9.6.2   Bias and just representation   178
     9.6.3   A just allocation of health-care resources   179
     Notes   180
     References   181

Epilogue: Democratization and the Changing of Professions   182

  Some History   184
  Democratization   185
     Shifting power and inclusivity   185
     Commercialization   186
  Transforming Society and the Professions   187
  Notes   189
  References   189

Index   191

Acknowledgments

I am indebted to the many students and working professionals who have, over the years, helped me to explore and better understand the issues discussed in this book. I also am thankful to colleagues for serving as a sounding board for ideas. And I am especially grateful to Hugh LaFollette, whose encouragement and good editing were instrumental to my engagement with professional ethics.

Introduction

Opening Thoughts	2
Being and Acting Professional	5
Definition and Listing	6
Cases	7
Note	10
References	10

──────────────── Opening Thoughts ────────────────

I was recently enjoying lunch with a couple of high-ranking police officers when the following exchange took place:

OFFICER ONE: What are you working on these days, Christopher?
ME: A book on professional ethics.
OFFICER TWO (*LAUGHING OUT LOUD*):   Oh, as opposed to amateur ethics? I'm really good at those!
OFFICER ONE: Heck, I'm just trying to be better than a *novice* at ethics – haven't quite made it to amateur status.
OFFICER TWO: Is there someone I can pay to be an ethics professional?

Good chuckles ensued all around, but their clever play on words captured a key problem with the topic of this book – just what do we mean by *professional* ethics? Consider the following statements, all of which rely on a different meaning of the term:

- "Muhammad Ali became a professional boxer in, after fighting for six years as an amateur."
- "That painter sure did a professional job, don't you think?"
- "Prostitution is the world's oldest profession."
- "You can count on Jones gardening: we are the most professional in town."
- "Sam sure is a professional complainer."
- "Did you hear Gabriela passed her licensing exam and is now a professional engineer?"

You probably recognize each of the different senses and have probably used several yourself. Despite some clear overlap, the meanings attached to the different uses vary so much that no single ethics conversation could effectively apply to all – the specific ethical duties attached to professional boxing, for example, differ widely from those of engineering.

This book focuses on the last meaning, that is, on the *formalized* sense of professional. It does so for two reasons. First, the other meanings all derive from the last in that they appeal to some version of a higher standard, one worthy of additional pay or respect. Even the fifth usage gets at the idea that Sam is a *really good* complainer. That is, they are at least loosely tapping into the common understanding that to be a professional is to possess a normative commitment to higher quality.

Second, the very goal of this book is to make explicit that normativity, the moral foundation at the core of professionalism. In short (for now), the thesis of this book is that to be a true professional, unlike other economic activities, is to be dedicated to a client relationship grounded in *trust*: trust in the professional's competence and in her commitment to place the well-being of her client at the forefront of their encounters.

Think of it this way:

You're in the market for a new car so you go to a local dealership, settle on a model, and, after some haggling, agree on a price. Thrilled with your shiny new toy, you happen to run into your buddy Omar a few days later who, lo and behold, has just bought the same model! In discussing the options you each purchased, Omar says, "I guess you didn't read the Consumer Reports review." You agree that you didn't and he goes on to explain that they concluded this model doesn't need such add-ons as rust coating, an extended warranted, or sealcoat paint – all items that you now realize you got suckered into buying by the very persuasive salesman. You also learn, to your great annoyance, that Omar also paid considerably less for his, even taking into account those add-ons.

Now compare that story to this one:

A month later you go to visit your orthopedic surgeon to discuss the pain in your knee. She explains that it's almost certainly torn cartilage and orders an MRI to confirm. It comes back positive for a very small tear, one that's still attached to the original meniscus.

Upon discussing your options, she persuades you to undergo a procedure in which she will remove the torn piece and also shave the underside of your kneecap to remove any rough spots. That shaving will cause some real tenderness for at least a week, during which time you'll need to be on crutches – which her office is only too happy to sell you, along with special compression socks and bandage wraps.

You agree to proceed and all goes as planned. You are on day six of recovery, still on crutches, when you have dinner with your cousin and her new husband, an orthopedic surgeon. Naturally the conversation turns to your injury and you explain your procedure. The more you talk, the more surprised he looks, until he finally cuts in and says, "I truly hate to tell you this, but the standard of care for the type of tear you have is not to operate. Rather, the goal – so long as you can deal with the discomfort – is to leave everything intact, since removing cartilage often leads to later arthritis. Further, while such kneecap shaving can help in extreme cases – that is, when there is significant malformation – from everything you've described, your situation doesn't even come close."

What would be your respective reactions to these cases? If you are like most, in the first you'd be angry and annoyed – partly at the salesman, but even more at yourself for not doing your homework. You *know* that the salesman's goal is to make as much off the sale as possible, just as yours is to get it as cheaply as possible. You even thought you'd done a pretty good job in the haggling; realizing that you haven't, you kick yourself and vow to do better next time.

In the second, however, wouldn't you feel deeply *betrayed*? You thought you could *trust* the surgeon to know what she was doing and not to be trying to make extra money off you. After all, you were dependent on her to help you with something really important: your health and mobility. What was that license on her wall about if it was not a guarantee that she was a *professional*?

The surgery case is intentionally extreme, to pull out the key differences between strictly commercial or instrumental dealings and fiduciary ones. In the former the primary motive of both parties is self-interest; each is trying to gain something off the other. Done well, both sides gain, but one knows to approach them with eyes open; *caveat emptor* – buyer beware – is the basic rule of the game.

In fiduciary relationships, by contrast, while self-interest is also present, the foundation of the relationship is a *partnership*, one intended to help you meet a vital need. In this type of encounter, you are dependent on the surgeon to be an expert and to treat you in a manner that places your well-being at the forefront. In return, you have committed yourself to treating her with respect, including being honest and forthright in your interactions and compensating her fairly for her work. When that trust is broken, you feel particularly betrayed – by her and by the system that granted her the authority, and the state *license*, to work as a physician.

As we shall see in subsequent chapters, any number of factors have arisen over the last few decades that challenge this somewhat idealized model of professional ethics. Still, even if it has become clear that clients in professional/client relationships should also do their homework – if for no other reason than that it is unlikely the professional will sufficiently know what is most important to you, what your most vital needs are – it is still the case that, as a general rule, you can in fact trust professionals more than you can trust someone who is merely in it for the commercial transaction.

Being and Acting Professional

Importantly, however, *being* a professional is not the same as *acting professionally*. Not all those who meet the formal criteria (see Chapter 1) always act with expertise and in their clients' best interest. And, of course, many of those whose work does not entail any of those criteria do their work with great integrity and treat their customers fairly and with dignity and respect. On the former point, as I write this there is a disturbing essay (Anonymous, 2015), with accompanying editorial (Laine et al., 2015), in the *Annals of Internal Medicine* that describes abhorrent medical behavior, clearly beyond the pale of any ethical human encounter, let alone a professional one.

That it *was* professionals (the story describes sordid actions committed by two senior-level physicians), that is, people to whom are entrusted that which is most important to individuals – in this case, the patients' bodies – makes it all the worse. But it also made headlines precisely because they were committed by professionals and were thus by far the exception to the rule.

This book will show why such behavior *is* the exception. In Part I, I describe how a professional norm rooted in deep ethical standards emerged, largely as a way of distinguishing professionals from pretenders, a move that also came with the great economic benefit of a monopoly on practice. I also recommend a model of ethics reasoning for addressing tough ethical problems, one based upon some of the classic approaches to ethics theory. Part II, the bulk of the book, explores some key concepts (e.g., role-engendered duties, conflict of interest, and competency) and their connection to core problems in professional ethics. In the Epilogue I discuss how the idealized model of professionalism has undergone major transformation as part of a society-wide movement that "democratized" key institutions. Some of these changes have been for the good – enhancing, in particular, client autonomy and informational power; some have caused serious ethical damage, for example, the commodification of the professional–client relationship.

Definition and Listing

Before engaging all those topics, however, we need a working definition of "profession" in order to capture a meaning that incorporates the core standards that distinguish formal professions from other occupations or jobs. Hence: *To be a professional is to be an expert, skilled at the provision of vital services, while also holding a normative commitment to their clients' well-being.*

Chapter 1 provides a brief history of the emergence of that definition, with emphasis on the development of formal professions. I show how these activities both naturally emerged in response to increasing complex social systems and were artificially designed for the mutual benefit of professional and client. The argument in this chapter also makes it clear that the professional/non-professional distinction is too stark. We're really talking about a continuum in which some occupations clearly fit the criteria, some are in the process of formally professionalizing, and some meet the criteria more or less marginally (or not at all). Again, though, being a professional does not guarantee that one will treat their clients with dignity and respect (or vice versa); the characterization is partly historical, partly sociological, and partly an exhortation – a reminder to those who fit the criteria that they are engaged in a *calling*, dedicated to a vital social service, with corresponding social and economic rewards and associated duties.

One last point about terminology: the words "ethics" and "morality" are also subject to multiple uses and meanings. For example, many folks think of "morality" as something very personal, connected to family and religion, while "ethics" is more objective, connected to social structures or organizational settings. In philosophy we generally use the term "ethics" to mean the application of moral theory, both of which are potentially objective. I follow that meaning here, to the point that there are places where the terms are used near synonymously.

Cases

Here are three cases to think and talk about as you read the next couple of chapters.[1] Consider, in particular, what makes them cases about *professional* ethics and not just ethics problems generally, and see if you can reach some consensus on how they should be resolved.

Health-care professionals and the conscience clause

California, like nearly all states, has explicit legislation that grants health-care professionals the right to exempt themselves from the provision of services that violate their conscience. California also provides a positive right to health care for all wards of the state (e.g., state and county prisoners), including the right to all legal reproductive services. It tasks counties with providing the medical care necessary to fulfill that right. This obviously has the potential to create a catch-22. On the one hand, counties are legally obliged to provide, for example, abortion services, but it is possible that all qualified physicians will exercise their right to conscience-based exemption (Meyers and Woods, 1996).

You are the new head of the California licensing board and have been presented with a petition to amend the existing conscience clause to make it harder to obtain an exemption. (Current law merely requires the professional to state that he or she has an "ethical, moral, or religious objection" to participating in the provision of those services.) You are seriously considering it, but are deeply torn. You recognize that being a physician in California is a privilege, one that comes with tremendous social benefit and correspondingly strict role-based duties. But you also find it troubling to demand that someone participate in a medical practice that he or she finds morally objectionable.

How should you resolve this conflict?

Defending the indefensible

You are a licensed attorney who handles almost exclusively criminal defense cases. You are approached by the family of a man who has been charged with a particularly brutal rape and murder. You strongly consider declining – right now you just don't have the emotional energy to manage this high-profile and very public case – but the family convinces you that the charges are a racially motivated travesty of justice (the suspect is African American, the victim a young white). You meet with the defendant and immediately establish an affectionate rapport. The more you talk and the more you investigate the case, the more persuaded you are that he is in fact being rail-roaded and you are very confident that you will be able to convince a jury.

You go to meet with him the day of opening arguments, however, and it is like he's a different man: angry, spiteful, he uses foul language and is abusive toward you and the guards who ushered him into the consultation room. After just a few minutes he says, "You know I did it, right? That bitch was just a tease who deserved everything she got. Thank goodness you're such a hot lawyer who's gonna get me off." Five minutes later, though, he's back to being the sweet gentle man you've come to know.

You are sickened, literally retching, at this turn of events. But you also recall that the psychological evaluation you ordered early on found nothing unusual and you know that the judge will never let you recuse yourself at this late date, given the prejudicial impact that would have on the already seated jury. You can't throw the case – doing so would violate your role-based duty to zealously represent your client and could get you disbarred – but you also can't imagine helping to put this guy back on the street.

What should you do?

Getting by with cheaper materials

You are the lead engineer on a public works project to rebuild a major bridge over a salt-water bay. The associated road is one of the busier ones in a very busy city. The traffic disruption will be severe, so the bridge has to be finished as quickly as possible. And, because it is a public project, the budget is, of course, very tight; your bosses (one of the nation's largest engineering firms) have made it crystal clear that the profit margin is tiny. In short, there is pressure from every quarter. If you screw up, there will be serious consequences; if you succeed, it will be a career-making project.

You are just completing final designs and overseeing the last of the major purchases. Sam, your purchasing manager comes to you and notes that you "just missed the window on the cheaper price for those high-quality bolts that we were ordering from the Swiss manufacturer. Evidently there's some major new undertaking in southern China and that firm has already put in a higher bid than we budgeted for. Because we were already in discussions, the manufacturer has given us the choice to match it and they'll complete the sale, but we have to decide by tomorrow. The new price, though, is a dollar more per bolt." You slump in your chair, knowing that cost puts you well over target. Sam explains that you could easily enough get lower-quality bolts produced, ironically, by a Chinese company, and they are even cheaper than what you had budgeted for the Swiss-made version.

You've already gone to your boss a couple of times to discuss budget and timing concerns; after the last meeting she forcefully said, "Look, Joe, I don't want to be bothered by all these details. They are your responsibility – please handle them yourself from now on."

You've heard mixed reports about the cheaper bolts. From all accounts, the vast majority are first rate, but the occasional one is reportedly of lower quality – low enough that they may not be able to hold up to the corrosive salt air. You talk with your assistant, another highly respected engineer, who says, "Come on, Joe. Going over budget is just not an option here and in this short time frame, I don't see where else we can cut corners. We're at the bone as it is. Get the cheaper ones – you'll look good for coming in *under* budget and you can just alert maintenance to keep an eye on them."

What should you do?

NOTE

1.   Many of the cases in this book are versions of, or inspired by, ones I have struggled with over my career. Identities have been altered to protect privacy.

REFERENCES

Anonymous. 2015. "Our Family Secrets." *Annals of Internal Medicine* 163 (4): 321.

Laine, Christine, Taichman, Darren, and LaCombe, Michael A. 2015. "On Being a Doctor: Shining a Light on the Dark Side (Editorial)." *Annals of Internal Medicine* 163 (4): 320.

Meyers, Christopher, and Woods, Robert. 1996. "An Obligation to Provide Abortion Services: What Happens When Physicians Refuse?" *Journal of Medical Ethics* 22 (2): 115–120.

Part I
Theory, Concepts, and Ethics Reasoning

Unlike some case-based approaches to practical or professional ethics, the assumption here is that one cannot effectively address ethical problems without two key foundations: conceptual clarity on core concepts and their relevance to different professional concerns; and a method for reasoning through tough ethics problems.

Part II is devoted to that conceptual analysis while here, in Part I, we will explore a reasoning model. First, we need to get a clearer picture of the general topic of professionalism. As noted in the Introduction, this book treats "professional ethics" as a distinct area within the broader categories of practical and theoretical ethics; that is, to study either of those fields is not necessarily to study professional ethics, given its narrower focus. See, for example, the extensive work in business ethics, where there is only limited overlap to concerns that are specific to professional ethics.

Thus, Chapter 1 provides a review of the historical circumstances that resulted in professions – not all societies have them, after all – along with the specific normative connotations that come with that status. From there, Chapter 2 develops a method of ethics reasoning. Emphasizing ethics *reasoning* is, admittedly, in contrast to the approach most common to ethics texts, wherein readers are introduced to key thinkers, that is, the "he argued, and then *he* argued, and then *he* argued" approach. Readers are shown why these great thinkers are so interesting and important, and then, in each case, given a list of reasons as to why the theory will not work. Connections between the theories are typically treated as mere contrasts, not as areas of agreement. This too often produces a kind of roller-coaster effect: students read Aristotle and are convinced that he is right, until they read Kant and find him conclusive, and then Mill, and Ross, and Rawls, and so on. It is no surprise then that students often give up on theory: "If these really smart folks can't get it right, who am I to try to figure out the correct theory?" Ethics reasoning is thus reduced to mere or ad hoc reactions or, worse, to naive relativism.

Here, the goal is to give readers guidance in genuine practical ethics reasoning, while also emphasizing the best insights of all the major theorists. It is hoped that these insights will give readers ample opportunity to rely upon the approach they find most valuable. But I also stress that the grand insights provided by each of the major traditions in fact complement the others far more than they conflict. The method urges that, carefully done, in particular with sufficient attention to the complex array of facts present in any ethics issue, those insights can be melded into a process for making sense of tough ethical problems, even for finding better *answers* to those problems – better if not always best answers. No method, to my mind, can guarantee the latter, but it can distinctly narrow the choices, excluding those that are clearly wrong, and give good reasons in defense of a few, often a very few, better ones.

Historical Overview and Definitional Questions

1.1	Some History	16
1.2	Defining "Professional"	23
1.3	A Working List	30
1.4	Types of Professional–Client Relationships	32
	Notes	35
	References	36

© Mike Baldwin / Cornered

"When you awaken you will feel fresh and relaxed – with absolutely no memory of changing my lightbulbs."

Not only are there myriad ways in which the term "professional" is used, but there has also been a marked increase – nearly 700 percent – in published instances of the term between 1800 and 2008.[1] It has clearly become a common part of our vocabulary, though with mixed meanings.

To see why our definition of professionals – as experts skilled in the provision of vital services, who have a normative commitment to their clients' well-being – is key to an understanding of professional ethics, it helps to get a sense of how professions formally emerged in history. This review shows that the process of formal professionalization occurred for two key reasons:

1. There were vital needs that existing service systems did not adequately address. Medical practice, as we shall see, serves as the paradigm.
2. Professionalization enabled the relevant groups to assure clients that they can trust that their practitioner had the relevant expertise and ethical commitment.

Both of these brought obvious advantages to clients. They now had skilled practitioners to whom they could turn for assistance with vital needs, and there was a greater likelihood that those needs would be effectively addressed. Practitioners similarly benefited. They acquired a monopoly over their services, with corresponding increases in wealth, social status, and power.

Those benefits also motivated any number of service-driven activities to *claim* professional status; even without the state-sanctioned monopoly of licensing, to call oneself a professional is to lay claim to an associated cachet, with its economic and status benefits. Too often, however, this was a mere declaration, without the requisite training, skills, and normative commitment that were associated with the profession. Consider the near-ubiquitous self-designation as "professional" by everyone from gardeners to hairdressers to, yes, car salespeople.[2] And it is at the heart of the familiar expression "Prostitution is the oldest profession." The idea here is the largely sardonic one that people have been willing to pay for such services for as long as there have been people. Regardless of whether the claim is historically accurate, prostitutes, as will soon become clear, meet very few of our criteria for professionalism, nor, for that matter, do most athletes, gardeners, beauticians, or car salespeople.

Furthermore, all too often even the groups that formally professionalized allowed power and status to get in the way of fulfilling their true professional commitments. This straying from the ethical foundations on which formal professions were built has led to a recent reinforcement of those foundations, demonstrated in reinvigorated ethics curricula in undergraduate and professional programs and books like this.

I acknowledge from the outset that our definition of a professional as an expert who is skilled in the provision of vital services and who retains a normative commitment to his clients' well-being – is somewhat artificial, especially given that the most common meaning in ordinary language attaches professionalism with *pay*: to be a professional, per ordinary language, is to be paid for those services. This is exemplified in the distinction between an *amateur* and a *professional* athlete in sports. The latter are paid to compete while the former do it, presumably, for the love of the game.

Although the compensation component is the most pertinent to the meaning employed in each of the examples noted above, there is also at least an implied understanding that the "professional" designation grants distinction. Such persons are *better than* their amateur counterparts; they have more experience-based expertise and are committed to an ethical norm that prioritizes clients' needs. In short, to self-designate in this way makes for great *marketing*. Such people believe, and probably rightly so, that when they promote themselves as professionals potential consumers of their services will at least unconsciously *trust* them to do well by them.

While such trust is often warranted regardless of whether the individual or company meets the formal criteria (section 1.2), there is no structural reason to *assume* that this going in, whereas with the formal professions, trust is the *default*. It is because the formal professions have emerged in human history in response to changing vital interests and with strict, carefully designed credentialing processes underlying their creation and continued practice.

That trust is often warranted regardless of formal status is, in fact, a key thesis of this chapter, indeed of the whole book. While our definition and associated criteria will allow us to easily identify definite professions, the concept will also admit of degrees, ranging from clear profession to marginal, emerging, or non-professional work activity. Furthermore, that someone meets the definitional criteria does not guarantee that she will always *act* professionally. I have, for example, known and worked with too many university professors who were at best marginally competent and who treated their student-clients as means to an end, whereas my long-time gardener is as skilled and as honest as the day is long; he has always done his job professionally, while those professors failed in the key normative criteria.

1.1 Some History

Backing up, then, who *were* the first professionals? Consider the root of the term "to *profess* about matters of vital importance." Hence the first professionals were spiritual advisers, who provided wisdom and guidance on an issue of, arguably, incalculable importance: one's relationship with the divine. And they did so from a socially sanctioned position of competent authority and thereby of *trust*. Their role also gave these early clergy social status; they were typically held in great esteem, often with the corresponding benefits of enhanced material comforts, features that continue to be common to contemporary professionals. Further, archeological records reveal that human cultures from the earliest times relied on such trusted and authoritative voices.

Once clergy – or more accurately, the learned, since members of this group were among the very few who received a formal education and were literate – started branching out into other areas of vital human interest, they sustained commitments to their original, if also evolving, religious foundations. For example, early medical practitioners, particularly in Egypt and the Far East, were as much religious clergy as they were physicians, and their medical practices were richly infused with religious ritual, side by side with empirically and scientifically developed cures. Early educators had a similarly religious focus. For all the noise about Socrates' impiety, the charges against him were mainly about his corrupting the youth about the *wrong* gods, not about turning them into atheists. Plato similarly infused deeply and richly religious themes into all his dialogues.

1.1.1 The rising role of science

While this continuing religious influence in increasingly scientific enterprises helped the clergy retain power and status, conflict was inevitable. By definition (most) religious activities are rooted in faith, not in science, or at least not directly so. From the earliest days, thus, religion and science have had to decipher how to coexist, with science playing an ever-increasing role. In ancient Egypt, for example, the spectacular monuments to the god-kings – pyramids, temples, and the Great Sphinx – were made possible only by highly advanced mathematical and engineering skills. Ancient Greece and Rome also struggled with the growing separation between appeals to the supernatural and increased understanding of how the natural world works. That understanding, not religious belief, was what allowed for the creation of the extraordinary infrastructure – plumbing, roads, bridges, buildings – without which Rome would never have been able to sustain its far-reaching empire. The men (all historical evidence suggests that they were pretty much exclusively men) who created these structures also enjoyed high social status and relative wealth; they were the equivalent of our upper management.

Although much of European culture and academia regressed during the Middle Ages, even as clergy reinforced their hold on power, these early specialists – essentially proto-professionals – maintained a presence, largely through informal apprenticeships. People still needed, after all, buildings, roads, and water. They also needed help with legal, medical, and animal husbandry concerns. Loose organizations thus began to emerge, eventually promulgating variations on what we later came to recognize as the legal, medical, and veterinary professions.

Throughout this entire period, religious authority had a solid stranglehold on socially sanctioned "truth." Correct answers came from understanding God's will and only those who were properly trained in liturgical interpretation – and in the literacy skills needed to access written scripture – could claim such understanding. Heavenly inspiration even extended to the selection of monarchs; they were understood to have been chosen by God and thus carried the "divine right" to rule as they saw fit (the story of King Arthur, with his divinely enabled removal of the sword from the stone, is a popular depiction of this idea).

1.1.2   Impact of the European Enlightenment

These beliefs ultimately ran head on into the European Enlightenment, with its astonishing explosion of culture, education, scientific discovery, and political transformation. Exemplified in the work of Copernicus and Galileo, the scientific turn came to fruition in the ideas of people like Francis Bacon, with his defense of science as the path to truth (Bacon, 2008), and John Locke, with his rejection of the divinely inspired monarchy (Locke, 1988). These great thinkers helped motivate societies to turn to the scientific method to make sense of the world and to the inherent dignity of all persons as the foundation for governing structures. Add to this that, thanks to Gutenberg, written material could now be widely disseminated and you have the foundations for a newly educated and politically engaged citizenry.

Furthermore, Europe also saw a dramatic population explosion in the eighteenth century as a result of increased life spans and improved infant health, which came with the reinvention of water and sewage distribution (the systems perfected by the Romans had largely been abandoned after the fall of the empire). The mushrooming social structures, particularly those concentrated in cities, became increasingly complex, with a corresponding need for people to manage the associated infrastructure needs, including legal and political arrangements, science, and education.

In short, these major societal transformations created a whole new set of human needs, along with the need for associated experts – a process that certainly continues today (consider, for example, the role of computing professionals relative to a mere forty years ago). The ranks of proto-professionals thus quickly expanded beyond clergy to include physicians, engineers, and lawyers. Further, while training for these proto-professions had previously been strictly through apprenticeship, universities increasingly took on that role, to the point that by the turn of the twentieth century, a college degree was considered the minimum prerequisite for professional training.

The largely mental expertise of these experts was both new to human society and in growing demand, enhancing their social status and economic standing even further. As with the clergy, the matters on which they practiced were of vital, if now more earthly, importance – for example, physical health, criminal and civil justice, and building safety. The client was thus deeply *dependent* on the expert: something critical to his well-being was at stake and he had little to no capacity to address it. Further, and again similar to the clergy's earlier position, he didn't even have the capacity to evaluate the expert's legitimacy other than through word of mouth and basic trust; the knowledge gap was just too wide.

It was no surprise that into that gap jumped opportunists, who were only too happy to take advantage of the fearful and needy. These schemers and scam artists – consider, for example, the origin of the term, "snake oil salesman" – claimed to have the same ability to fix your problems or cure your ills, and often far more cheaply. As often as not, though, they were just trying to swindle you out of your last dime.

1.1.3 Organizing to differentiate

Seeking a way to distinguish themselves from the fraudsters, those with legitimate proficiency determined that the best message was one of *structural* trust: "You can have confidence in us because we have created the structures – education, training, continuing oversight, and assurance of right character – that certify that we have the right skills and ethical commitment." These structures, and the formal bodies that came with them, provided a promise that their members were the real deal.

Medicine was the first to make this official move when the eventually named British Medical Association (BMA) was founded in 1832. Shortly thereafter, the association took on the role of determining the qualifications, including the right ethical standards, one must have to be deemed a physician. Not long after this, the association also developed the accrediting requirements for medical education in both classroom and residency settings. In short, the BMA was the first to create both the *credentialing* and the *curricular* standards that would assure the public that its members could be trusted.

The American Medical Association (AMA) followed suit in 1847, setting a normative stage at its inaugural meeting by establishing the association's first Code of Ethics. That act was intended to convince clients that its members were exceptional: it could be trusted both to have the requisite skills and knowledge *and* to have the promotion of its patients' interests as its primary motivation. It was also aimed at politicians, those who could, and soon would, grant it an economic and practice monopoly.

1.1.4 Formalizing the standards

Full adoption of credentialing and training criteria emerged in fits and starts, with the Flexner Report on US medical education (Flexner, 1910) serving as the key wake-up call for the need for strict nationwide standards. The result was a formal tightening of accreditation and apprenticeship requirements, producing the system of medical education, including residency programs, that we have today. Being a product of such a system, thus, gives one a kind of imprimatur: "You can trust me because I've received the system's approval." At the same time, the system motivated suspicion, if not cynicism, of those who were *not* members of the club. That suspicion was formalized when national and state legislators gave the AMA a monopoly over membership: they and only they could determine who should receive a license to practice.

The establishment of such confidence could occur, of course, only if members really *were* better, if the medicine they practiced was of a higher quality than could be found at the local barbershop.[3] This in turn motivated a more scientific approach to medical care and produced profound health-care advances, especially in pharmaceuticals. Hence we have ended up with a massive system, one that trains (both initially and through continuing education), ethically sorts and reinforces, self-regulates, and motivates the development of drugs and equipment.

To give a sense of just how enormous that system is, consider that the United States is expected to spend $3.35 trillion dollars on health care in 2016. That is more than $10,000 for every single person in the country. (Another way of thinking about just how much money we are talking about is to realize that you cannot count to even one trillion: assuming one number per second, twenty-four hours a day, it would take over 32,000 years to get to 1 trillion.) It should be no surprise, then, that even professionals of strong character and great training sometimes get seduced into pursuing profit at their clients' expense – a point we shall return to in the Epilogue.

1.1.5 Establishing trust

Even acknowledging the potential for corruption, it is important to recognize just how unusual and exceptional the professions' normative foundation is. Think about when you walk into your doctor's (or lawyer's or professor's or engineer's, for example) office. While you may have a healthy wariness, your overriding attitude is very likely one of *trust*. You trust them to know what they are doing – the license on the wall attests to those skills – and you trust that they are not going to order tests just to pad their bank account; instead, they will prioritize your well-being. Even though we generally take it as a given, such default confidence is in fact very striking; compare it, for example, with the attitude with which you likely approach a car purchase, where you assume that the salesperson is trying to make as much money off you as possible and, depending on local legal requirements, may not be fully honest about all a vehicle's quirks.

The vast majority of commercial relationships are, at their core, instrumental: each party is using the other to achieve an end, and suspicion about one another's motives is the norm. Hence, any modification to *caveat emptor* results from the parties having a pre-existing relationship, or is driven by the desire to create a long-term and mutually beneficial relationship, or is mandated by legal or regulatory oversight.

As we shall see, the structural conditions that create professional–client trust have taken some serious hits in the last few decades, but faith in the professional's basic normative foundation still prevails – and, for the most part, rightly so. That faith is the product of the *system* that socializes professionals through proper training, experience, oversight, and prioritization of client well-being; it is also explicitly present in the recognition that *individual professionals* have an ethical commitment to the relationship. They see their work as a *calling*, not just as a way to make a living; their very *identity* is largely defined by their professional role.

1.1.6 Monopolies, money, and power

The associated monopoly, however, along with the deep power asymmetry that typically exists between professional and client (one with expertise and exclusive access, the other typically vulnerable, fearful, and dependent) creates plenty of opportunity for abuse. Thus the formal arrangements established by the BMA and AMA had, from the outset, a built-in tension: on the one hand, they worked to protect patients' vital needs through the creation of real standards for what qualified as medical practice, while, on the other, they created an economic monopoly. The resulting power – legal power, knowledge power, and power rooted in sick or injured patients' vulnerability – made it easy for any given professional to exploit their status for personal enrichment, all while claiming a privileged standing. To balance this tension, the associations had to inculcate in their trainees, through classroom and especially residency training and mentorship, a deep commitment to a fundamental normativity. Physicians were socialized into thinking of medical care as a calling and to dedicate themselves to the highest level of medical knowledge and to an avowed commitment to placing patients first.

While this structurally normative approach was hardly perfect – many physicians abuse the tremendous power attached to their role – it was largely successful in distinguishing authentically professional health-care practitioners from charlatans, and it was *very* successful in creating social status and wealth for its members. It is no surprise, thus, that it became the model for other budding professions like law, engineering, dentistry, veterinarians, accountants, and psychologists.

As I shall discuss in the Epilogue, however, this history took a turn in the 1980s, as the professions became, in William May's terms, "beleaguered," challenged by clients insisting on more control, by governments increasingly distrustful of the professions' ability to successfully self-regulate, and by businesses wanting a larger cut of the lucrative pie (May, 2001).

───────────── 1.2 Defining "Professional" ─────────────

In his influential book, *Professional Ethics*, Michael Bayles argues that the definition of key concepts – like "professional" – should emerge empirically, via a review of how the term is *used* in ordinary discourse (Bayles, 1981). As we have seen, however, that ordinary usage is now so broad as to include everyone, from those who are merely compensated for their services to those who assert – often for marketing purposes – a higher level of expertise, to those who have gone through extensive training so as to provide expert service on vital matters.

Given that the very goal of this book is to identify the special ethical considerations that distinguish the traditional professions, the ordinary language approach is clearly too inclusive. Thus, I prefer a *conceptual* approach, one that makes sense of what distinguishes these activities, in part by building upon the understanding gained through the historical analysis of the preceding section. That analysis shows us that activities like medicine and law *became* professions by reacting to newly emerging vital needs and by formally defining the criteria necessary for being identified as a member of the group.

Central to those criteria is trust. The client must be able to trust the system to have granted an imprimatur only to those with proper training and character; he also needs to trust that a particular professional has the requisite skills and will not abuse her power by taking advantage of him emotionally, physically, or economically. He needs to trust that the professional is there *for him*, first and foremost, and not there just to make a buck. Professional colleagues also need a similar level of trust – again, in the system and in the individual – so as to feel confident about referrals or collaborative management of a client's problem.

For such trust to be present, a number of other necessary criteria must be satisfied, as they provide the structural conditions that make trust possible. Four of those criteria are *essential*, that is, all must be met, at least to a large degree, in order for the activity to be considered a formal profession. Others are common features that are typically present in traditional professional client relationships, generally as a consequence of the fulfillment of the essential criteria. Note also that there is a reciprocal relationship between the essential features and the core normative definition of trust that one's professional is a skilled expert committed to fulfilling clients' vital needs. The definition is *informed* by the criteria and at the same time *emerges* from them. That is, trust couldn't exist without the satisfaction of these criteria and, because professionals satisfy them, we trust them to assist with our vital needs.

1.2.1 Essential features

The activity must address a *vital need*. Vital needs include physical and emotional health and associated protection from factors – human and natural – that could threaten either; the freedom to pursue interests; economic stability; spiritual guidance; and education. Because humans value these so deeply, we feel particularly vulnerable when they are threatened. Hence the need for a genuine expert – a *professional*.

The members of the profession must receive *extensive education and training*. Some of the abilities necessary to be a competent professional – for example, empathetic engagement and listening skills – emerge from life experience and good parenting, but others come only through formal education and apprenticeship. Imagine, for instance, the deeply empathetic lawyer who does not know state law or who has not had training in courtroom litigation. All her care and compassion are worthless without the proper knowledge and skills and you would be foolish to place your liberty or economic security in her hands. All of the clearly identified professions, thus, require at least a baccalaureate degree and most also call for a post-graduate degree.

There must be *self-regulation* by the members of the profession, usually overseen by a professional organization, with associated credentialing. As we saw in section 1.1.3, the BMA and AMA (and, later, other groups) convinced legislators to grant them a monopoly over services by vowing to provide proper oversight of their members. Such oversight includes development of the standards that educational programs must satisfy in order to be accredited to teach professionals-in-training, determination of the knowledge and skills one must satisfy to receive credentialing or licensing, and punishment of licensed members who fall below the standards, in terms of either expertise or ethical character. Government agencies also review the associations' work, but final decisions are generally left to the professionals. For example, only other academics can determine whether someone has met the standards to be a tenured professor, only other attorneys can disbar a lawyer, and only medical societies can remove a physician's license.

In addition to the group authority and control granted by self-regulation, individual members also have considerable *autonomy* over how they practice. Although there are clear minimum standards that any professional must meet – for example, a professor must have knowledge of his subject area and a surgeon must have a good grasp of anatomy as well as the requisite physical skills; beyond that, individuals have profound flexibility over how they satisfy their client's needs. That flexibility is captured in the axiom that medicine (or teaching, litigating, programming, and so on) is as much an art as a science. The very best professionals supplement their factual knowledge with creative insight and judgment.

1.2.2 Common features

The professional–client relationships that have, over time, emerged from these essential criteria have also produced a number of common elements, including the following:

- A *monopoly* over services. This emerges directly from the self-regulating criterion. When legislators granted individual professions the authority to determine who can and cannot practice, they also thereby granted them a monopoly over those services. How far that monopoly extends is a constantly moving target. As I write this, for example, the California legislature is debating a bill that would significantly expand nurse practitioners' scope of practice into activities currently restricted to physicians or surgeons (e.g., ordering durable medical equipment, certifying disability for purposes of unemployment insurance, and having a more direct role in the treatment plan for home health patients). Similarly, a wide range of education and training organizations have made sharp inroads into the traditional universities' monopoly over college degrees.

  Still, the monopolies are quite strong. It is against the law to give legal advice if one is not a member of the state bar; only physicians may prescribe certain medications; and one must be professionally certified to perform key engineering activities. The monopolies even extend to control over how many students are admitted into postgraduate professional programs, in part to keep supply low enough as to increase eventual practitioners' *income*.

  And because these monopolies are so strong, with little to no plausible competition, the potential for *abuse* is correspondingly high. Professional associations can establish outrageous fee structures, cover for their own when faced with accusations of incompetence or inappropriate behavior, and establish relationships that produce real conflicts of interest in their fulfillment of client need. We shall discuss these and related concerns in later chapters.

- The work activities are largely *mental*. While professional activities sometimes require specialized physical skills (e.g., a surgeon's dexterity and an architect's drawing talents), most professional work is intellectual – hence the need for extensive formal education. That education also typically produces a *specialized* and *technical language* that is unique to the professional activity. Such language serves both as a type of convenient shorthand among practitioners and as a way of distinguishing members. Membership in the "club" is partly determined by one's facility with the terminology.
- The intellectual emphasis also contributes to higher *social status* and, again, *increased income*. Whether or not it is justified, society values intellectual more than physical activity and compensation levels generally follow. The "vital activity" component of professional work also contributes to higher compensation, of course. The *responsibility* attached to holding someone's heart in one's hands, someone's freedom in one's arguments, or the structural integrity of a bridge in one's design warrants greater recompense.
- There is typically a strong *power asymmetry* between professional and client. This is structurally rooted in the very purpose of the relationship. The client needs help with a vital concern, help that he can get only from a professional. He is thus vulnerable and deeply dependent on the professional. He is likely also fearful, confused, and out of sorts because of the alien nature of the professional's everyday territory (one's first experience with an intensive care unit, for example, can be daunting indeed).
- The asymmetry is also created and maintained in the artifices – *the trappings of power* – built into professions and professional–client relationships. Notice, for example, the first thing that you see when you walk into a courtroom: an elevated judge's stand. The reason for that, no doubt, is partly the need for visual awareness of the courtroom, but it also serves to reinforce the judge's power (as do, of course, the "all rise" command, the black robes, and the requirement to address the judge as "your honor"). Similarly,

most of us would be uncomfortable calling our physician (or professor, for that matter) by her first name; "doctor" is more common, even while she is being far more informal with us.

These power trappings can be beneficial. A close friend once told me how reassuring it was, how it gave him a sense of confidence, when the physician treating his dying wife came into the room in a crisp white coat, with a stethoscope wrapped around his neck. However, they can also damage communication and reduce client autonomy; for example, note how frequently the professional interrupts the client and vice versa.

- Professionals generally see their work as a *calling*, as opposed to a job or even a career. Their lives are largely committed to the work and they typically *self-identify* as a professional. They recognize that they are assisting others with vital matters and see their work as providing a *service* as much as earning a living. This contributes to their willingness to fulfill special duties (see section 1.2.3), including – for the traditional professions, at least – a willingness to be *on call* twenty-four hours a day, seven days a week.

1.2.3 Role-based duties

As the preceding discussion shows, there are many privileges attached to being a professional, most notably high social status and enhanced compensation. Those privileges, combined with the core normative commitment to serve others in their vital needs, in turn produce a set of general role-based duties, as well as specific ones connected to the professional's particular role.

First among the *general* duties is the overarching commitment to have one's *clients' needs* as the highest priority. Trust is possible only if clients can be confident that their professionals are not satisfying their own interests at the cost of their clients'. It is also possible only if the professional accepts the duty to treat all his clients as persons worthy of dignity and respect. This translates into such specific role-based duties as *informed consent* requirements and respect for *confidentiality*.

Prioritizing client needs also extends to the commitment – in the right circumstances, with the right considerations at stake – to provide a professional service to those who cannot afford to pay for it. Most professional associations have a requirement of some kind of *pro bono* service. The New York State Bar, for example, recently determined that fifty hours of *pro bono* service is a prerequisite for admission to its bar, and the California Bar is considering a comparable requirement. Similarly, the service component for university tenure and promotion decisions was originally meant to capture this ethos of giving back, though these days it is largely about campus rather than community citizenship.

Another general duty is the commitment, noted earlier, to be *on-call* twenty-four hours a day, seven days a week. Most professionals now operate as part of a group, so such call requirements are managed on a rotating basis (or, in a hospital setting, by house staff). But solo practitioners still recognize that they can be called in the middle of the night to assist a client in need. Not all professional activities carry that kind of urgency but the requirement is still loosely present in *work schedules and hours*. For example, while it is rare that a college professor will need to take a 3 a.m. phone call,[4] very few work a standard forty-hour week; the work needs (class prep, grading, etc.) dictate the hours and schedule. I know of no professors who do not at least sometimes work at night and on weekends, and nearly all work at least fifty hours a week.

Sticking with the professor example: her list of specific role-based duties is too long and context dependent to list here, but includes such obligations as *remaining current* on information and techniques, *being available* to meet with students or colleagues, *respecting data privacy*, and, like health-care professionals, providing *informed consent* through a syllabus and maintaining *confidentiality*. The key point here is that the roles we adopt in life – professional, occupational, parental, friendship, and so on – all bring with them particular duties. If we fail to fulfill these roles in personal relationships, we are generally no worse than lousy friends or relatives; if we fail them in a professional context, given the vital needs at stake, we can cause profound harm.

One of the more challenging aspects of professional ethics is that role-based duties sometimes conflict – with one another (e.g., a contractual duty to one's firm conflicting with a fiduciary duty to a client) or with one's other central values (e.g., a pharmacist's duty to dispense legally ordered prescriptions, say RU 486, with his religious beliefs regarding contraception or abortion). Chapter 2 provides a method of ethics reasoning that can help resolve such ethical conflicts and in Chapter 4 we will discuss conflicts of interest and obligation.

1.3 A Working List

Any list of the professions is bound to be contentious, so I focus here on those that clearly qualify, in alphabetical order:

architects
licensed attorneys
ordained clergy
dentists
engineers with Professional Engineer (PE) certification
physicians (including psychiatrists)
licensed pharmacists
professors
licensed psychologists
certified public accountants
veterinarians.

Each non-controversially fulfills all the essential criteria and each is deeply, if sometimes only generally, committed to the normative foundation of client trust. The democratization movement (see Epilogue) has made that commitment harder to sustain, but all these professions retain it, along with the other essential criteria.

Those that qualify as *marginal* professions fall along a continuum, with some largely satisfying the criteria but not sufficiently so, and others meeting them only in a limited way. In descending order, the following are some prominent examples:

- *System administrators*: Aspects of the computing field are in the process of formally professionalizing (Guzdial, 2013) and system administrators will certainly be among the first who qualify. They provide a vital service and are highly educated, with extensive and specialized training. For now, however, they don't have either an authoritative mechanism for certification or a sufficiently strong commitment to client well-being. There is often, in fact, no clearly identifiable client at all.

- *Scientists*: Those who are also college professors, or who have the relevant terminal degree and work for a public service agency (typically government related), satisfy all the criteria. Those who work for profit-based businesses likely meet all the technical criteria but may have just too deep a conflict of interest (see Chapter 7) to be able to fulfill the core normative criterion. Part of the difficulty here lies in determining who the client is. As with journalists and ethics consultants (Meyers, 2007), professional scientists have no distinct person as their client. Rather, the "client" of scientific activity is something like "the truth" and those whose loyalties are divided between that pursuit and the profit-making needs of the corporation cannot generate the level of trust necessary to unconditionally meet professional standards.

- *Nurses*: Their commitment certainly aligns with the normative core (client well-being as their highest priority) and most consider their work to be a calling. But their individual and group autonomy is largely constrained by the medical hierarchy, and educational levels vary significantly – ranging from associate's degree to a doctorate. *Physical therapists* and *chiropractors*, while generally highly educated and committed to the primacy of client needs, are in many ways even more constrained by medical power (depending on the laws of the state).

- *Teachers*: Much like nurses, they care deeply about their clients and they generally see their work as a calling, but they have limited power or autonomy over instructional methods and, especially, curriculum. As I write this, the "Common Core" initiative of the Obama administration grants more freedom to teachers to motivate critical thinking skills in their students, but that freedom runs head on into the ongoing demands for high standardized test scores.

- *Journalists*: Journalists have lost much of the public trust they acquired during the Watergate era. Surveys now consistently place them among the least trustworthy of occupations. And, while they are almost wholly autonomous and highly skilled (if not technically so), journalists need not have any formal education. Nor are they subject to licensing or formal regulation beyond that given by their editors. And, as with scientists, it is not at all clear who their client is. The public? Their publisher or station owner? Other journalists? The truth?

Other fields are becoming increasingly professionalized worldwide and likely will move into the formal ranks in the coming decades, including higher ranks of military and public safety officers, other disciplines in computing (e.g., advanced programmers and hardware designers), and various occupations within the arts (e.g., museum curators and composers or conductors).

——— 1.4 Types of Professional–Client Relationships ———

A last consideration is whether there is a single ideal relationship for every professional–client encounter. The short answer is no: different people – even the same people in different circumstances – have differing goals and capacities. Thus no single relationship type fits everyone. Among the more important requirements, in fact, for the ethical professional is the need to evaluate which type is appropriate in what settings and with what people. Let us consider some of the options, with their respective strengths and weaknesses.[5]

Recall that people go to a professional because they have a significant need. The professional is presumably well trained and able to provide expert advice or technical skill in relation to concerns of vital importance, including the promotion of client well-being and autonomy. The best ways to satisfy these mutual needs can vary tremendously, with options ranging from strongly authoritative to mere agency. I list five commonly cited options here; some place greater emphasis on client well-being while others prioritize autonomy.

1.4.1 Agency

In these relationships the professional serves primarily as the client's agent, helping him to achieve his already established goals. Picture a client who routinely gets sinus infections and knows that he needs an antibiotic to clear them up. His physician serves, in these instances, as the legal facilitator for the client, since he cannot get a prescription without her help. Such relationships work well only when the client is sufficiently knowledgeable (and the professional knows this) and the professional does not object to being treated merely as an agent. Note also that it probably will not work on complex issues, wherein the very expertise that distinguishes the professional is vital to finding mutually agreeable solutions.

1.4.2 Paternalistic (or parentalistic)

The converse of the agency relationship, paternalistic or parentalistic ones put all or most decision-making authority in the hands of the professional. The client concedes authority, trusting the physician to have sufficient expertise, commitment to client well-being, and the experience and judgment to choose wisely.

Dominant prior to the democratization movement of the 1960s and 1970s, paternalistic relationships are now widely criticized in the ethics literature. Given, however, the wide power asymmetry between professional and client, along with client fear and dependency, varying degrees of paternalism are still commonly present in professional–client encounters. And they can be highly effective when client trust is present and warranted; that is, when the professional genuinely has the requisite expertise and wisdom and is truly committed to the client's well-being – *and* when they take the time to acquire enough information about what is important to the client. This turns out, in fact, to be one of the most significant impediments to paternalistic relationships. The professional assumes that he knows what a good outcome would be – since it is what *he* would want – without sufficiently exploring the client's short- and long-term goals.

1.4.3 Contractual

In these relationships the client and professional hold closely equal power and they work together to agree upon a mutually acceptable course of action. And, as the term suggests, they rely on *legal* sanctions to enforce the agreement. That reliance, of course, suggests a starting point of reduced trust; it also assumes a very informed client and the professional's willingness to treat the interaction in largely transactional terms. This type of relationship is more common in such fields as engineering and architecture, where power symmetry is more frequently found, and less common in health care, education, and criminal law.

1.4.4 Affinity

These relationships are deeply rooted in trust, but trust based less on standard professional roles as on shared values, background, or faith. Since life plans vary so significantly, this approach holds, it is foolish to assume that one's professional will genuinely understand one's goals – unless they come from a similar value frame. As Robert Veatch (1981) suggests, the ideal professional arrangements would include, for example, faith-based hospitals where all the health-care professionals have very similar religious beliefs and corresponding values. This would give potential patients the ability to choose to receive care from people whom they can be confident will at least largely share their world view.

While affinity relationships built upon previously existing friendships are quite common, the broader framework Veatch recommends suffers mainly from economic constraints. It is just not feasible to have that many service locations (most religiously based health-care settings, for example, hire people from a wide range of belief systems) and insurance plans would have to grant sufficient latitude to choose where one wants to be treated. Another challenge is that the affinity must itself be grounded in morally valid beliefs. Members of criminal gangs or of terrorist groups, for example, have affinity relationships within their group.

1.4.5 Fiduciary

In many respects the ideal model, these relationships are grounded in a *partnership* in which professionals and clients each have duties and responsibilities and each *trusts* the other to act accordingly. The client recognizes, for example, that the professional brings superior technical knowledge, while the professional recognizes that the client has individualized values and life goals. They thus work together to achieve the best mutually desired outcomes.

While ideal – done correctly, a fiduciary relationship could largely look like an agency or a paternalistic one, if that is what works best in the specific circumstances – fiduciary relationships are also among the toughest to achieve. Clients must have sufficient self-understanding (see Chapter 3) and professionals must be able to overcome the range of constraints and inducements that undercut trust.

Each of these relationships has its advantages and disadvantages and each will be appropriate for some people or for all people in some circumstances. To bringing it back full circle, one size does not fit all and the ethically committed professional will strive to achieve the one that is most appropriate to a specific person and her needs.

NOTES

1. https://books.google.com/ngrams/graph?content=professional&case_insensitive=on&year_start=1800&year_end=2015&corpus=15&smoothing=7&share=&direct_url=t4%3B%2Cprofessional%3B%2Cc0%3B%2Cs0%3B%3Bprofessional%3B%2Cc0%3B%3BProfessional%3B%2Cc0%3B%3BPROFESSIONAL%3B%2Cc0, accessed August 21, 2017. Some of what follows is taken from Meyers (2015).

2. Association of Professional Gardeners (www.associationofprofessional gardeners.org, accessed August 21, 2017); "Beautician: Educational Requirements To Be a Beauty Professional" (http://study.com/articles/Beautician_Educational_Requirements_to_Be_a_Beauty_Professional. html, accessed August 21, 2017); Car Sales Professionals (http://carsalesprofessional.com, accessed August 21, 2017).

3. Barbers were among the earliest (if only marginally competent) surgeons – hence their red and white poles, representing the rags that hung outside their shops in medieval Europe.

4. Early in my career I received such a call after having my students read an excerpt from Albert Camus's *The Myth of Sisyphus*. The student was convinced that Camus's life-affirming answer to the opening question – whether we should commit suicide – was mistaken. Happily, the student ultimately changed his mind and went on to enjoy a flourishing life.

5. Some of what follows is motivated by a similar analysis provided by Faber (2003).

REFERENCES

Bacon, Francis. 2008. *Francis Bacon: The Major Works*, edited by Brian Vickers. New York: Oxford University Press.

Bayles, Michael. 1981. *Professional Ethics*. Belmont, CA: Wadsworth.

Faber, Paul. 2003. "Client and Professional." In *Ethics for the Professions*, edited by John Rowan and Samuel Zinaich Jr., 125–134. Belmont, CA: Wadsworth.

Flexner, Abraham. 1910. *Medical Education in the United States and Canada: A Report to the Carnegie Foundation for the Advancement of Teaching*. http://www.carnegiefoundation.org/sites/default/files/elibrary/Carnegie_Flexner_Report.pdf, accessed August 21, 2017.

Guzdial, Mark. 2013. "What's Our Goal for a CS Degree, and How Do We Know We Got There?" *Communications of the ACM*. http://cacm.acm.org/blogs/blog-cacm/166032-whats-our-goal-for-a-cs-degree-and-how-do-we-know-we-got-there/fulltext, accessed August 21, 2017.

Locke, John. 1988. *Two Treatises of Government*, 3rd ed. Cambridge: Cambridge University Press.

May, William F. 2001. *Beleaguered Rulers: The Public Obligation of the Professional*. Louisville, KY: Westminster John Knox Press.

Meyers, Christopher. 2007. "Clinical Ethics Consulting and Conflicts of Interest: Structurally Intertwined." *Hastings Center Report* 37 (2): 32–40.

Meyers, Christopher. 2015. "Professional Ethics." In *International Encyclopedia of Ethics*, edited by Hugh LaFollette. Hoboken, NJ: Wiley-Blackwell. http://onlinelibrary.wiley.com/book/10.1002/9781444367072, accessed August 21, 2017.

Veatch, Robert. 1981. *A Theory of Medical Ethics*. New York: Basic Books.

2 A Model of Ethics Reasoning

2.1	Relativism, Absolutism, and Contextualism	40
2.2	Deontology	43
2.3	Utilitarianism	48
2.4	Context, Context, Context	51
2.5	Ross and Pluralistic Deontology	53
2.6	A Model of Ethics Reasoning	57
2.7	Moral Principles	63
2.8	Case: Cutting Corners	65
	Notes	66
	References	66

The Professional Ethics Toolkit, First Edition. Christopher Meyers.
© 2018 John Wiley & Sons Ltd. Published 2018 by John Wiley & Sons Ltd.

It was dawning on Ed that maybe his
conscience wasn't such a good guide after all.

Imagine the following scenario. It is the end of the semester and you are getting ready to enter final grades when a student stops by your office. You recognize her as having received an F in the class and brace yourself for what you expect to be a plea for mercy. Unlike most such pleas, however, she begins by acknowledging that she has not turned in her final paper and thus, per the standards on your syllabus, deserves a failing grade. She asks, however, "Is there nothing I can do at this point? The paper is mostly done, but I couldn't complete it because my father was in a bad car accident last weekend and we were all in the hospital, giving him support." You offer sympathy but remind her that on the syllabus and in class you have made it clear that you are open to accommodation in unusual cases, but only if the student contacts you prior to the due date, otherwise she receives a failing grade. She agrees that you made that crystal clear, but "I was totally focused on my dad and just couldn't think about my classes." She notes that this is her last term and that she needs to pass the class to graduate (her only other professor agreed to let her take the final exam late so that she could pass that class) and asks for a few more days to complete the paper. You look through your grade sheet and note that she'd done fine up to the paper, receiving solid Bs on all previous assignments. Should you give her an incomplete and let her turn in the paper late? Or should you stick to the clearly spelled-out rules on the syllabus and encourage her to retake the course next term?

It might seem that there is an easy answer here: "Rules are rules and we must apply them equally to everyone; if I were to give you an extension, I would have to offer the same to all the other students." But are there ever cases in which the rules should be adjusted to accommodate other moral considerations, including, here, the negative impact on the student? Or can one argue that the prevailing rule in this case – formal justice – should be overridden by *another* moral rule, here, beneficence? How do considerations of character inform your choice; for example, how might your revered grad school mentor have handled the request?

Note that the option you adopt, the way you answer each of the questions, represents an endorsement of a model of ethics reasoning. The "rules are rules" approach aligns with a strict deontological view; concern for impacts with some version of consequentialism; a balancing of rules with mixed deontology; and character questions with virtue theory.

In this chapter we shall briefly explore each of these, building on the assumption that theory informs better moral reasoning, and conclude with a suggested method for working through tough cases, one that melds together insights from each of those classical theories.

— 2.1   Relativism, Absolutism, and Contextualism —

First, however, we need to think about the *kinds* of answers we reach when we engage in ethics reasoning – in particular, what truth value they have. Are they correct only for the person who reaches them?

Or for his immediate culture? Or are they true for all persons at all times, or maybe for any persons in a similar moral circumstance?

The personal and cultural approaches represent types of relativism. The first, more extreme, version is called *subjectivism*. It holds that ethics "truth" is nothing more than the beliefs or preferences of the individual stating them. It is like saying "Hot fudge sundaes are good." The second, more moderate, version is social or cultural relativism. It holds that ethics truth is reducible to the norms established by the larger social group in which one resides, with such groups ranging from relatively narrow (e.g., one's sorority) to quite wide (e.g., "Western society").

While there are plausible, if also very sophisticated and complex, versions of social or cultural relativism, the more common versions – and certainly subjectivism – can be easily dismissed. First, as Mary Midgley (1981) convincingly argues, the kind of tolerance relativism demands of us also precludes *any* evaluations based on normative standards. If each culture's (let alone each person's) views are as good as any others, we would have *no grounds* upon which to criticize any of its practices – nor would it have any grounds upon which to criticize ours. In fact, we would have no objective grounds for criticizing even subcultures within our own; that is, we would have no *standards* for such a critique beyond that we just do not like it. One can quickly see that in such a framework power (or the loudest, most obnoxious voices) would prevail – hardly the foundation for healthy and productive social engagement.

Second, despite the hand waving we often give to relativist positions – after all, we teach our children every day to respect, or at least tolerate, others' religious and cultural views – very few of us actually believe in a more comprehensive version. For example, imagine how you would react if you encountered someone who thought it was perfectly acceptable to torture children for the fun of it. Granted, the odds of your ever coming across such a person are slim to none – such psychopaths are, thankfully, rare indeed – but if you did you would undoubtedly consider them truly *evil*.

But *why* would you? Surely it is not the same kind of reaction as you would have if you were to encounter someone who does not like hot fudge sundaes (horrifying as such a prospect would be!). No, your moral evaluation would be far deeper and far more definitive.

Third, it turns out that, according to anthropologists, there has never been a society that tolerated such gratuitous harm; all known human cultures have deemed it immoral to harm innocent others simply for the fun of it. Now, there has assuredly been profound disagreement over what counts as "harm" and about when it makes sense to consider others as "innocent." We even regularly disagree about *who* counts in the equation, that is, what sorts of beings should be recognized as persons worthy of moral respect. In short, cultures differ widely on what count as legitimate grounds of justification for harmful actions, but note that they all think that justification is necessary. Why? Because gratuitous harm is obviously wrong, so one must somehow justify the harms one causes.

On the other end of the spectrum are the absolutist approaches, those that hold that correct moral claims must apply to all persons at all times. As we shall see in section 2.2.1, Immanuel Kant is among the most famous – and respected – representatives of this position. He concludes, for example, that lying is always wrong, both because a rule that promotes dishonesty cannot be universalized and because the person who is lied to is being treated as a mere means, as an object and not as a person. Various religious traditions adhere to similarly absolutist views, placing unqualified prohibitions on everything from the intentional killing of innocent humans, to divorce, to suicide.

One can certainly see the temptation in observing such black and white, all or nothing, positions: they take the work out of ethics decision making. One need only know the rule and make sure one follows it categorically. ("Categorical imperative" is, in fact, the label Kant gave his overarching moral rule – categorical in that it applies to everyone at all times, and imperative in that it is a moral *command*.)

The problem, though, is that life does not seem to divide out into neat black and white choices. Rather, every day brings choices that seem to fall in the gray zone, everything from the trivial ("How do these pants look on me?") to the profound ("Please, doctor, you cannot tell Mom about her cancer; if she finds out she'll give up all hope and never make it to her grandson's wedding in three months") to the life-threatening ("Should a woman be prohibited from ending the life of the fetus conceived by rape whose continued existence threatens her own life?"). That is, we are faced with a range of choices for which there are at least very strong intuitions that the absolutist stance cannot prevail; there is just too much at stake to hold on to the rule dogmatically.

But if we give up on absolutism, does that push us back into relativism? Not necessarily. A middle position, one that will be explored in greater detail in section 2.4, is *contextualism*. On this view, the rules have powerful but only conditional moral force. Thus, for example, one should do all one can to be honest, to avoid deceiving others, but if honesty butts up against other equally powerful moral principles, say not causing harm, there will be any number of cases in which morality demands that honesty be overridden. And on some versions of contextualism, for example that of W.D. Ross, if we have done our moral reasoning properly – including due consideration of outcomes and character development – the resulting decision is the universally correct one, for all persons in morally similar contexts.

2.2 Deontology

Nearly all moral theories are concerned with *the right* and *the good*. The right typically refers to the means by which moral agents make their choices, whereas the good refers to that being sought or promoted. Deontological theories, by and large, focus on the right, consequentialist ones on the good. Thus, for deontologists, agents' *motives* are key considerations, as good ones are core to acting rightly. So long as one is choosing and acting for the right reasons, deontologists argue, one is being moral, even if bad results emerge. Said differently, moral responsibility is attached to motives, not to outcomes.

The thinking here is that *why* we act is all that is fully within our control, whereas outcomes are susceptible to informational deficits and an uncooperative reality. We cannot reasonably, thus, hold someone accountable, deontologists argue, if he rightly acted on the best available information, even if it turned out to be inadequate or false, with correspondingly bad outcomes. And, by the same token, if one intends to do evil but accidently produces good, one has still acted immorally (e.g., an assassin attempts to murder the president but inadvertently strikes a terrorist before the latter can release a devastating biological weapon).

Thus the key to acting rightly, for the deontologists, is acting upon principle. They believe that there is an inherent moral force in principles, which creates a duty to abide by them. The source of that moral force varies: some believe that God provides it (see the Jewish and Christian Decalogue, Islam's Moral Commandments, or Hinduism's Achara), others that reason demands it (see Kant), or that morally mature persons intuitively know it (see Ross).

Note that non-deontological systems will often have their own set of rules, but the key difference is that, in those theories, the rules are *only instrumental*. For example, in rule utilitarianism, we should abide by the rules because they tend to promote the good being sought – they are good predictors of outcomes – and not because they have inherent moral value.

2.2.1 Immanuel Kant

Kant is the best known of the deontologists, in part because he was a brilliant philosopher with very compelling arguments, but also in part because his views are often seen to be too extreme. A brief overview does not do him justice, but let me capture some key points and urge interested readers to seek greater detail in this book's predecessors, *The Philosopher's Toolkit* (Baggini and Fosl, 2010) and *The Ethics Toolkit* (Baggini and Fosl, 2007).

First, even though he was a devout Christian, Kant did not believe that God's existence – let alone specific religious or moral tenets – could be rationally proven. His goal, thus, was to answer a number of key questions in philosophy, including morality, without appeal to religion.

Second, Kant believed that morality's core is found in *accountability*, in the recognition that, in the right circumstances, people should be held responsible for their choices. To say that someone should be punished (or rewarded), however, assumes two key conditions: that she must be free to choose otherwise and that there must be known standards that apply to everyone equally.

Kant's argument for *freedom* is famously difficult but here's a short version. Kant believed that rational agents, persons, have dual natures: a strictly mechanistic ("phenomenal") nature – our bodies and our personalities – that is, like all other mechanisms, subject to the laws of cause and effect; and a non-mechanistic ("noumenal") nature – our will and our capacity to reason – that is outside the bounds of those laws and is capable of being a first cause.

The metaphysics here are certainly problematic, but they should look familiar if you come from any of the religious traditions that see our bodies as mere vessels for our souls. Within those traditions bodies are also seen as being subject to cause and effect – including decay and eventual death – whereas the soul is wholly free and permanent.

On the *standards* condition, Kant argued that morality demands "universalizability," standards of evaluation that apply equally to all persons at all times and in all circumstances. Thus even if one is dealing with a masochist one should not accede to his request to self-harm, since, Kant's rule demands, we must do not what persons contingently *want* but what can be rationally applied across the board.

Without universal standards, he concluded, morality becomes little more than subjective preference statements or empirical surveys of what people in fact do or say. But since he had already rejected a theological source for universalizability, he turned to the only other known example: *reason*. Look at mathematics or formal logic, Kant says: correct answers in those realms hold true across all possible circumstances; truth and falsity are absolute, *necessary*, and totally devoid of subjective or relativistic intrusion.

Moral decision making must therefore be rooted in and fully constrained by the rules of reason. This sounds plausible enough, but look deeper and realize that he means that our moral choices must be driven by reason *alone*; no subjective considerations can influence our choices. This includes emotions, relationship-based loyalties, personal histories, circumstantial contingencies, or even consideration of consequences, since those are not necessary but merely contingent.

Hence, as noted earlier, we get the troubling conclusions that it is always wrong to lie (even, infamously, to the murderer at the door), that one cannot allow emotions to alter our duty (we have no greater moral requirements to a loved one than to a stranger), and that it is always wrong to break even a trivial promise (even if keeping it means ignoring an injured person in need of help). In each of these cases, Kant argued, the alternatives rely upon considerations that cannot be universalized (mere predictions of beneficent outcomes in the lying case, subjective emotions toward loved ones, and the contradictory implication of a "contingent promise") and, without such universalizability, accountability fails.

Again, many consider some of these conclusions to be at best problematic. To focus on the last, how can it be that morality would demand that I keep my promise to meet a friend for coffee rather than tend to an injured person in need of my competent assistance? Kant sticks to his guns in the face of such critiques, arguing, first, that one should not make trivial promises and, second, that one cannot know with certainty that rendering aid will produce better consequences than meeting the friend. In one sense, the first response is compelling: we should probably reserve promises for major issues, giving mere "assurances" instead in less demanding cases. In another sense, it is unrealistic: people *will* make promises with the sincere intent to fulfill them, even if they do not always do so with the level of technical care and formality that Kant's dictates would demand, in particular with sufficient knowledge of and attention to the range of considerations that could impede such fulfillment.

The second response is considerably more troubling. Even if we cannot *know*, deductively, that stopping to help will produce good results, inductive reasoning surely tells us that the likelihood is extraordinarily high. Said differently, and in the way Ross takes up (see section 2.5), even when we are careful in our commitments, our duties – here, fidelity versus beneficence – will sometimes conflict with one another and only by carefully evaluating the contextual contingencies can we determine what our most pressing duty is.

For all these problems, however, Kant certainly revealed several key insights about moral reasoning. First, we should seek at least a reasonable standard of impartiality in our moral choices. Even granting greater role-based duties to, among others, family members, we should strive to evaluate those duties as equitably as possible and, everything else being equal, treat all others as moral equals. Professionals cannot justify, for example, giving preferential and higher-quality treatment to some clients merely because they enjoy their company more than that of others.[1]

Second, motive surely counts. We have a higher moral regard for people who intend to do good than for people who are fundamentally egoists and who just happen to accidently end up benefitting others, and correctly so, even if we occasionally fall short,.

Third, one of Kant's key conclusions and one not explicitly addressed earlier, is that persons – those beings who can engage in rational moral evaluation and have the freedom to act upon resulting choices – are *special*; they are holders of *dignity* and are thus worthy of profound moral respect. This conclusion – captured in the best known of his versions of the categorical imperative – "Always treat persons, oneself included, as ends in themselves and never as mere means" – lies at the core of a wide range of professional ethics requirements, everything from informed consent to writs of habeas corpus, to requirements to be forthright with clients.

I will incorporate these insights into the method for ethics reasoning discussed section 2.6.

2.3   Utilitarianism

Whereas deontological theories emphasize *the right* (i.e., the process one undertakes to make moral choices and the intent the agent has), consequentialist theories focus on *the good* (how we best promote desirable outcomes). The best known and most respected of the consequentialist approaches is utilitarianism. In contrast to Kant's complex metaphysics, utilitarianism is quite straightforward. It starts with a naturalistic claim that humans (and, more recently, all sentient beings) wish to avoid physical and psychological pain and to seek pleasure.

2.3.1   John Stuart Mill

As Mill's declares in his famous credo, "Actions are right in proportion as they tend to promote happiness; wrong as they tend to produce the reverse of happiness. By happiness is intended pleasure and the absence of pain" (Mill, 1979, 7). One's moral duty, simply put, is to strive to take those actions that are more likely to make the world a better place, via an aggregate balancing of pleasure over pain.

The complexities emerge in determining what counts as pleasure (or pain) and how to measure those differences. Mill's predecessor and mentor, Jeremy Bentham, argued that one should focus primarily on the physical, in part because emotional or psychological pleasures and pains can be reduced to how they make one feel *physically*. He then contended pleasure and pain can be directly measured through a kind of hedonistic calculus. When faced with, say, a governmental policy choice, one should, in his view, plug it into a seven-step calculus and act on the choice that produces the greater aggregate pleasure.

While agreeing with Bentham's general strategy, Mill believed that pleasures and pains were not so easily quantifiable. The pleasure one gets, for example, from reading poetry is mainly *qualitative* and, in fact, of greater worth than the merely physical (though Mill certainly was not arguing that the physical should be ignored). Thus, when making, say, resource allocation determinations, one should prioritize qualitative pleasures, including educational opportunities, since they are pleasurable in their own right and since they give one the ability to properly distinguish between types of pleasures.

Even if this qualitative approach makes determinations in specific cases problematic – there is no simple calculus to which one may appeal – it more fully captures the range of human experience and of what we naturally value. Furthermore, Mill notes, it is unusual to have to fret too much over specific cases. Millennia of human existence have taught us some basic rules of morality, such that when we follow them there is a far greater likelihood that we will produce aggregate pleasure. Unlike with Kant, however, it is not that these rules have some inherent moral power but rather that following them will most likely satisfy the principle of utility. History has shown, in short, that violations of those rules generally lead to worse outcomes.

As we shall see, that "inherent moral power" conclusion will represent a point of departure for Ross and for the model of ethics reasoning that I shall eventually recommend. Ross (and I) argue that moral rules (or "principles" or "duties") are in fact intrinsically compelling; they place demands on us that are independent of the goods and harms produced by following them.

Another key problem for utilitarianism is the so-called problem of justice. Simply put, the theory seems to imply that the ends, if they are the right ones and of sufficient worth, will always justify *any* means taken to achieve them. And if the primary moral duty is to produce the greatest aggregate good, the most pleasure over pain, this might best occur with the sacrifice of an innocent individual. Any number of science fiction stories have been built around this idea, that an unlucky but innocent person must be sacrificed so as to appease some, usually unrevealed, great threat, thereby protecting the whole community.[2]

Mill devotes most of his primary ethics text, *Utilitarianism*, to responding to the theory's critics, with all of chapter 5 dedicated to these questions of justice. He argues that individuals' choices best promote utility when there is a commitment to, among other considerations, equal treatment: "All persons are deemed to have a *right* to equality of treatment, except when some recognized social expediency requires the reverse" (Mill, 1979, 61–62). Said differently, acting justly is far more likely to produce aggregate good.

But what of those "except" cases? Mill acknowledges that they can exist but he also plausibly claims that they would be rare, even extreme, since sacrifice of the minority would almost always produce disutility for the majority, via such indirect harms as reduction of social trust, increased fear, breakdown of relationships, and so on. For example, earlier in the chapter he talks about slavery being unjust because ultimately it will be "inexpedient," inconsistent with the principle of utility, because of the *corollary harms* associated with the practice (Mill, 1979, 45).

Does the extraordinarily rare exception represent a fatal error in the theory? First, it is not at all clear that strict deontological theories are in better shape. Even if one's intuitions strongly lean toward it always being wrong to sacrifice an innocent person for the well-being of the whole – in Kantian language, to use that innocent person as a mere means to the benefit of others – can one without hesitation say that such a violation is *worse* than terrible and widespread harm? As troubling as it is to accept the sacrifice of one so as to produce great benefit, or avoid great harm, we would also find it *just as* troubling, Mill says, to give up on that potential benefit for the sake of the one.[3]

A commitment to a strict interpretation of this aspect of the principle of justice is one of the core considerations that distinguishes an absolutist Kantian approach from Millian-style consequentialism, and one's intuitions here might well determine one's theoretical orientation. If either choice feels unpalatable, you might be drawn to a Rossian, pluralistic deontology, model in that he successfully splits the horns: justice, he says, is just one (very important) principle among many, and thus it must be weighed against other principles with which it is in competition. But even on a Rossian model there will be cases, truly rare cases, where any choice seems unacceptably wrong. Rosalind Hursthouse characterizes such cases as "irresolvable, tragic, dilemmas" (1999, 71–75). In such – thankfully rare – cases, there are many *bad* choices but maybe no single, ultimately correct one. We shall return to the question of dilemmas in section 2.4.

A last point on utilitarianism: as noted in passing, contemporary utilitarians (Singer, 2009) point out that, since the proper moral end is enhancement of pleasure and reduction of pain, humans are not the only beings to whom we owe moral consideration. Most animals, and certainly all mammals, have varying capacities for experiencing pleasure and pain and thus we have a duty to include their welfare in our utilitarian calculations. This is relevant to professional ethics in a number of areas, with experimentation for medical research among the most compelling.

──────────── 2.4 Context, Context, Context ────────────

Among the many merits to utilitarianism is its insistence that one must take the specific facts of the case into account when doing ethics reasoning. By contrast, on a Kantian approach one can develop the proper rules in relative isolation, by appeal to reason only, and then simply make sure to properly implement them in life's choices. For the utilitarian, and, as we'll see, for the pluralistic deontologist, only the general principles exist in abstraction, independent of the concrete realities of daily life. Best ethics choices can be made only by taking into account the variables of the case in question. While a rule utilitarian relies upon a kind of shortcut to such accounting, one must still consider whether the specificities of the case compel one to step outside those rules, forcing the agent to attempt to calculate the aggregate good in that specific case.

This recognition of *context* also informs Ross and his pluralistic deontology. As we saw, for Kant there are no genuine moral dilemmas: either the recommended choice comports with the categorical imperative or it does not. Ross thought that this black and white approach simply runs afoul of real persons' real moral lives. Consider the simple example from earlier: attempting to fulfill your promise to meet a friend at a certain time for coffee, you are rushing to get there when you encounter an accident where you can easily and effectively render life-saving aid to an injured victim. On a strict reading of Kant, it would be immoral to stop, since in doing so you intentionally violate your promise, thereby violating the categorical imperative. By contrast, Ross says, our moral lives are full of dilemmas, situations in which acting upon one choice – in this case, keeping a promise – conflicts with another moral duty – here helping another in great need.

But how are we supposed to figure out what the right answer is? This case is intentionally presented as an easy one. If you can stop to help, you surely have a greater moral duty to do so, rather than to fulfill your relatively trivial promise for coffee. But, add any complications to the story – your friend is in great emotional turmoil and there are others who could also stop to help the accident victim – and uncertainty soon emerges. For the Kantian, that uncertainty must be avoided at all costs; ethics reasoning, recall, should produce the same degree of necessity as mathematical reasoning. And the utilitarians largely agree: if one could accurately predict *all* morally relevant consequences to emerge from a choice – making sure that one has taken into account all those who will be affected (i.e., not reducing utilitarianism to egoism) – one could say with certainty what the best choice is.

Ross, by contrast, embraces uncertainty, at least with respect to determining the correct answer in any given case. Because we are "not omniscient" (Ross, [1930] 1988, 32), all our practical choices involve "moral risk": "We come in the long run, after consideration, to think one duty more pressing than the other, but we do not feel *certain* that it is so" (Ross, [1930] 1988, 30–31; emphasis added). In this regard he is like the humble utilitarian who concludes that our duty is to produce aggregate good, but who does not feel certain that any given action will achieve this. For both camps there is a recognition that reality, and especially human social interactions, are messy, involving a tremendous amount of guesswork.

That experience also rings true for the humble experienced professional. She is routinely faced with ethical dilemmas – conflicting options between competing principles, virtues, and goods – and she does the best she can within her position of epistemological uncertainty. That is, the reflective professional recognizes that ethics decision making is often a complicated business, frustratingly devoid of mathematical certainty. She has the choices, thus, to accept that messiness and commit herself to doing the hard work to get it as best she can, to abrogate her normative role as a professional and leave the decision making to others, or to (falsely) hope some rule book will provide all the answers.

2.5   Ross and Pluralistic Deontology

The title of Ross's book – *The Right and the Good* – reveals from the outset that he is trying to bridge the perceived gap between deontologists, who think morality is primarily concerned with the right (correct processes and motive) and consequentialists, who are mainly concerned with the good (producing the best possible outcomes). Although he is clearly a deontologist, Ross argues that ethics decision making *has* to take consequences into consideration, as revealed in the importance he gives to non-maleficence (avoid causing harm) and beneficence (do good), both of which are clearly forward-looking, consequentialist kinds of principles.

How do we know he is a deontologist? In three ways. First, even non-maleficence and beneficence, despite their consequentialist standard, have, he says, *inherent moral force*. They are binding on us simply because morality dictates it. Second, Ross also says that we must adhere to a number of backward-looking and thus deontological duties, for example fidelity and reparation. They are deontological because they are built upon actions we have already taken, rather than on outcomes we are trying to achieve. Last, he reminds us that making a promise changes our moral relationship, even if no significant consequences are attached. Imagine making a promise to a dying person, a promise no one else is aware of and whose fulfillment does not make the world a better (or worse) place in any way or significantly impact your character (Meyers, 2003). Do you have a duty to keep your promise simply because you made it? He thinks it is clear that you do, prima facie; that is, you should keep your promise unless some other overriding duty conflicts, for example, if keeping it could cause great harm. The consequentialist in such a case, that is, one in which there is no benefit or harm produced, must conclude: "Why bother? If neither choice impacts the aggregate good, either is acceptable." Ross says we *should* bother exactly because the very making of the promise changed our moral standing, creating a prima facie duty to abide by its terms.

His list of principles is knowable, he says, to all "mentally mature" persons (Ross, [1930] 1988, 29), who simply come to recognize them as true features of the universe. Such recognition comes through life experience – for example, by seeing what happens when someone breaks a promise or is treated unjustly – but it is not as if one can go and *look* for the principles in the world. Rather, they are discoverable in the same way as mathematical truths are and, he says, they have the same kind of certainty. That is, even though we can rarely be sure that we have the correct answer to a specific practical ethics problem, we *can* be certain that we should not hurt folks without good reason. We should also be honest, keep our promises, help others, be just (both in giving people what they deserve and in distributing scarce resources); further, we should be grateful and work to repair the harms we cause and should also strive to make ourselves better people.

How do we know these duties? He simply says they are "self-evident" (Ross, [1930] 1988, 31), again, like mathematical and logical propositions. This claim of self-evidency, combined with his reluctance (inability?) to provide *some* form of proof, has resulted in his being labeled, often disparagingly, as an "intuitionist." For some, the appeal to intuition is not a problem. Such people see the duties as simply an unexplainable part of the fabric of the universe – maybe provided by God or maybe part of the nature of reality in the same way that reason arguably is. Others say that there must be some way of justifying the duties and have appealed to, among other positions:

- a Rawlsian "veil of ignorance" (ask yourself, for example, whether you can *imagine* successful human relations that aren't rooted in moral foundations along these lines) (Rawls, 1999);
- a model of reflective equilibrium (reliance on these duties coheres with the range of other facts, beliefs, and theories that we accept to be true); and
- a version of evolutionary naturalism that shows how adherence to them has given humans a reproductive advantage (Meyers, 2011).

Much of the work in professional ethics has side-stepped these meta-ethics questions and simply accepted that we have a moral duty to abide by these principles, or a set of principles very familiar to it (Beauchamp and Childress, 1979). From there the question has been how to resolve ethics dilemmas, that is, when two or more of the principles conflict. Again, unfortunately, Ross is largely unhelpful here. He merely says that the circumstances of the case, through which one may determine the extent to which the duties are at stake, will dictate which should prevail:

> It may be objected that our theory, that there are these various and often conflicting types of *prima facie* duty, leaves us with no principle upon which to discern what is our actual duty in particular circumstances … [but] I would contend that in principle there is no reason to anticipate that every act that is our duty is so for one and the same reason. Why should two sets of circumstances, or one set of circumstances, not possess different characteristics, any one of which makes a certain act our *prima facie* duty? When I ask what it is that makes me in certain cases sure that I have a *prima facie* duty

to do so and so, I find that it lies in the fact that I have made a promise; when I ask the same question in another case, I find the answer lies in the fact that I have done a wrong. (Ross, [1930] 1988, 23)

Despite what many see to be significant gaps in his theory, Ross's keen insights nicely add to our method of ethics decision making. He reminds us that this is a messy business; that dilemmas are prevalent in daily life; that we have to give attention to what has happened in the past *and* in how our actions will impact the future; and that persons of good character embrace these challenges and do the best they can, accepting the "moral risk" that only an omniscient being could avoid, while being secure that moral blame is attached only to weak or insincere efforts and *not* to unforeseeable negative outcomes.

So how do we engage all these difficult challenges? Ethics decision making is not like a cookbook or a logical algorithm, but there *are* steps that can better ensure more ethically successful choices.

"John's in charge of advising us on ethical matters, but to be honest, I've never had much confidence in him!"

——————— 2.6   A Model of Ethics Reasoning ———————

The downside of working through the classical theories is that one might be tempted to come away from the conversation as a skeptic about whether ethics theory has any role to play in daily decision making.[4] If minds as great as Kant, Mill, and Ross could not come up with a workable theory, maybe we should just wing it?

The approach urged here is that such skepticism is misguided. Most textbooks present these theorists as isolated, even in opposition. And there is no question that, taken as a whole, a Kantian approach is in conflict with a Millian one, which is, in turn, in conflict with a Rossian one, and so on. But, if we do some cherry picking, building upon specific insights provided by each, a workable method emerges, one that that helps us reach better ethics choices.

There are any number of effective such methods (Elliott and Ozar, 2010; Gert, 2005). The one provided here is my preferred method, both because I have found it to be of practical value in resolving difficult, real-world moral problems and because it seems to do justice to these thinkers' great insights.

Thus, from Kant, we take the idea that we must treat all persons – however that concept is best understood (e.g., whether it is inclusive of some non-human animals and, potentially, artificial intelligence) – as *ends in themselves*. This means that one must have extraordinarily powerful moral reasons in order to be justified in violating their basic rights, for example to life, to liberty, and to physical integrity. It also means that, everything else being equal, we must be *consistent* in our application of moral standards. We also take from Kant that *motive* matters; it is, in fact, the key criterion for determining moral *accountability*.

From Mill we take the insight that *results* also matter: our duty to *help* others can be at least as great as our duty not to cause others harm or to maintain fidelity (see Chapter 4). We also take his key distinction between *qualitative and quantitative pleasure*: our efforts to make the world a better place must include the promotion of physical pleasures, for sure, but it should also prioritize intellectual, artistic, and emotional pleasures.

From Ross we take the recognition that these important moral concerns, these principles, will routinely come into *conflict* and that we must have a mechanism for determining which should prevail. In a related vein, Ross also informs us that we have to be *equally* concerned with the right and the good: right method, including right motive, largely dictates moral accountability, while effective decision making produces the good, successfully making the world a better place, in small and large ways.

None of these insights mean anything, however, if we are not committed to being *good people* – people who care about our moral relations with others, who are willing to undertake the often difficult work to get it right and who will have the courage to act on resulting conclusions. These are the lessons that Aristotle taught us nearly 2,500 years ago and that virtue theorists have been reinforcing ever since.

Virtue theory has, in fact, seen a major revival in recent years, in part because of its vital contribution to professional ethics. As we have seen, being a professional requires strength of character, including discernment, judgment, and understanding so as to make better technical choices and to better act on behalf of one's clients. Such strength of character is acquired through experience and, even more critically, through apprenticeship with role models, with the masters in one's field (see, for example, formal apprenticeship programs in medicine and architecture and informal ones in engineering and law).

As a reminder, ethics decision making is not about following some line-by-line recipe; there are multiple paths to better answers. Further, and again as a reminder, there will (nearly) always be important facts to which we will not have access and thus our choices will routinely involve some degree of moral risk. Accepting this means we will often have to settle for a narrow range of acceptable choices (and a *very wide* range of unacceptable ones), rather than holding out for certainty. That is, we may not reach the single correct answer every time, but we will assuredly discover a plethora of actions *not* to take.

2.6.1   A method and steps

We start with three general claims:

- Moral decision makers must begin with a *core commitment* to achieving the ethically best choice, even if that does not necessarily align with the prudentially best one.
- What counts as flourishing, as Aristotle argued, is always going to be relative to the economic, historical, and physical circumstances of the persons in question. A flourishing life for a twenty-first-century Californian is radically different than for a twelfth-century Saxon.
- The ethically best choice is one that achieves convergence between:[5]
  - best outcomes, in particular those that enhance individual and group flourishing and that create aggregate benefit over harm;
  - character promotion – again, individual and communal – through choices that serve to reinforce persons of honor, who are worthy of emulation; and
  - adherence to mid-level and lower-level ethical principles.

To reiterate: Ethics reasoning is not like following a recipe; it demands hard, creative, and, most importantly, *committed* analysis and evaluation. In any given case, one must first accurately determine the facts, after which the specifics of the case will dictate which of the following steps should be followed, in what order, and with what degree of intensity. Hence, this list should be treated as a guide and not as a strict procedure.

1. Determine the facts, especially the morally relevant facts. This might seem to be the most obvious step, but it is frequently both the hardest and the most likely to be done badly. It is the hardest because the facts often will include those entwined in institutional politics and in the "scripts" that guide how participants make sense of their world (Werhane, 1999). It is often done badly because a full elucidation of the facts is time consuming, often

difficult to achieve, and rife with potential conflict. What you take to be an obvious fact another may consider to be ideological bias (consider, for example, the fact of climate change).

Accurately and thoroughly determining the facts is the first step in the process because, more often than not, perceived ethical conflicts are really just disagreements or confusions about what is factually at work in the case. For example, a family might *hear* that a given treatment will likely produce a successful medical outcome, when the physician *meant* that success is possible, but chances are very slim. Getting all relevant parties on the same factual page frequently allows the dilemma to disappear.

Thoroughly understanding the facts is also important for moving past false perceptions of relativism. Facts will vary within different social and institutional contexts, including, for instance, how much value members of that community give to specific harms or goods. Examples here include the worth members place on such values as loyalty, respect for elders, or individual effort; the role of religious beliefs in members' engagement with problems; and how the community has legally codified its values. These and the many other related factual considerations do not change *the underlying principles*; they just change the ways in which those principles are seen to be at stake in the respective cases.

2. Determine what *type* of conflict it is, as these prescribe best responses. Options include:

    a. Moral distress, wherein one knows the best (or better) answer but is prevented from acting upon it because of power structures, the law, or economics. In these cases, one should seek to level the playing field, for instance by bringing in another person with power (e.g., an independent ethicist) who can advocate for the correct choice. Managed well, the problem should be resolved with such intervention.

    b. Moral ignorance, wherein one is in all-new moral territory and does not even know how to begin the evaluation. In such cases, one should seek the wisdom of others with more experience and/or seek wide-ranging input from persons from varied backgrounds, and then proceed to the next steps.

   c. Moral dilemma, wherein one has the classic conflict in which
       any choice will violate one or more of the principles, cause
       harm, and make it hard to be virtuous. In these cases, proceed
       to the next steps.
3. Determine *who* will be impacted by potential choices, that is,
   determine who is at stake and how they will be affected by available options. Note that this includes consideration of the relationships between the various players: how *deeply* will someone be
   impacted by a choice (e.g., the difference in impact by a spouse
   and a co-worker)?

   Similarly, what sorts of relationships exist between the professionals? For example, does the city editor have a history with
   the online editor such that he is (maybe unconsciously) looking
   for an excuse to cause her harm? Are there hierarchical power
   structures at play, for example where a more knowledgeable person is reticent to challenge someone with more clout? In short,
   how do all these relationships and histories inform the facts of
   the case?
4. Determine what general and role-specific principles are at stake
   in the problem. General principles are those that, per Ross, all
   mature persons recognize as being prima facie binding on us;
   role-specific ones are those that are motivated by the particular
   professional obligations inherent in that role, for example,
   obtaining informed consent, or being a mentor for a student (see
   section 2.7).
5. Determine *the extent* to which those principles are involved.
   Might, for example, respecting a professional duty to look out for
   the well-being of a client conflict with a general duty of honesty
   (for instance, by being "expansive" on a diagnosis so that a patient
   can get insurance coverage) and, if so, which is a more egregious
   violation? Which action will more likely produce an environment
   in which persons, individually and communally, can flourish?
   How does the choice impact the character of the decision maker
   (and, for that matter, of the recipient)? Has a range of morally
   imaginative options been considered, with the goal of seeking
   the best, most creative solution? How likely is it that proposed

solutions can be effectively implemented? What impact do organizational cultures, ideologies, power relationships, and so on, have on the implementation question?

Step 5 clearly represents the crux of the decision-making process, but it cannot even be entertained without a thorough analysis of Steps 1–4, especially Step 1. The complexities involved in determining the "extent" in which answers also reinforce how difficult ethics reasoning can be. The demand here, thus, is for moral agents to be active, engaged, and sincere in their deliberations and to do their very best within the practical and epistemological limitations that are likely constraining the ability to make the ideal choice.

6. Once the best available choice is made, determine what obligations, if any, emerge as a corollary to the decision. For example, if the case dictates, say, that one must harm another so as to respect an obligation of fidelity, does that produce a corresponding duty to try to repair the new harm?

7. To the extent that it is possible, see the choice through to its conclusion, including making sure that it is properly implemented. A key component to this final step is a corresponding commitment to transparency, what Rawls called a "publicity requirement" (1999, 48–49). Are you willing to share the decision you made and how you reached it, with whoever may ask?

Note how the steps combine to help one achieve the noted convergence between results, character, and principles and thus pull together the key insights from Kant, Mill, Ross, and Aristotle. They also emphasize that the nature of the relationships impacts on how the principles are at stake, thereby pulling in a key aspect of contemporary "ethics of care" approaches.

Will the steps guarantee the right choice? No, but they will likely improve your reasoning processes and thus make it more likely that you will get there. Let us test it. Try applying the method to the following case and see how confident you are that you have reached the right choice.

——————————————— **2.7 Moral Principles** ———————————————

- *Dignity*: Persons should not be used as mere tools. This includes respecting their status as autonomous agents. Persons as moral agents hold a status that demands a level of moral protection not afforded to other beings, even those who have considerable, if lower, moral status. It also means that we are able to hold them accountable for their choices. Captured in both the Kantian and contemporary notions of autonomy, the principle demands that we treat persons as morally relevant beings whose life plans and choices, as well as their desire to flourish, must be honored and even promoted (as feasible). Despite the frequent conflation of autonomy and mere *choosing* in practical settings (e.g., the belief that a signed form suffices for autonomous informed consent), autonomy is more about the development of, and opportunity to fulfill (changeable), life plans (see Chapter 3).
- *Non-maleficence*: It is wrong to cause harm for no moral reason. In order for an intentional or negligent harm to be justified, one must be in pursuit of a competing good and must do all one can within one's power to mitigate any concomitant harm. Some harm is often inevitable when one is acting on behalf of another principle or promoting other goods that will contribute to flourishing; this principle demands that the balance must favor that principle or good (see Chapter 4).
- *Fidelity*: One should keep one's promises, whether they are explicit or when any reasonable person would interpret one's actions and circumstances as implying such a vow. One also has greater duties of loyalty to those with whom one has an established relationship (see Chapter 8).
- *Reparation*: One should attempt to repair harms caused to others, whether directly (e.g., fixing, or paying to have fixed, the actual damage) or indirectly (e.g., providing cash restitution). The duty of reparation includes both harms that are caused intentionally or through gross negligence and those resulting from ignorance or carelessness, with the former placing greater demands upon moral agents.

- *Formal justice*: One should give to persons what they have legitimately earned and apply corresponding social structures (laws, civil rights) in an unbiased manner, that is, in a manner that takes into account only relevant factors, not arbitrary ones. The obvious application of this principle is via justice systems, but it also carries across to social benefits and privileges like licensing, marriage covenants, and educational opportunities (see Chapter 9).
- *Beneficence*: Persons should do what they reasonably can to improve the situation of others. "Reasonably" here refers both to problems of diminishing return (if one gives too much, it undercuts one's ability to give at all) and to the level of sacrifice that it is realistic to expect of persons (see Chapter 4).
- *Gratitude*: One should show appreciation for others' actions that are intended to be for your benefit. "Appreciation" can range from mere expressions of thankfulness to gifting in a manner comparable to the good provided. Full gratitude also accounts for the aggregation of enduring support or care, for example in a parent–child relationship.
- *Distributive justice*: While relevant at the personal level, distributive justice places its greatest demand upon the community to determine how to allocate social goods, for example access to power, wealth, and education – that is, more generally, the conditions that contribute to a flourishing life (see Chapter 9).
- *Honesty*: One should strive to avoid deceiving others, whether overtly or covertly. The key criterion is whether one knowingly and intentionally communicates in a way that results in others believing information one knows to be false. This distinguishes deception from ignorant communication of falsehood and it reveals that deceptive communication can fall along the continuum of overt and malicious, to covert and done with the goal of aiding or preventing harm to others, to self-deception (see Chapter 8).
- *Self-improvement*: One should endeavor to improve oneself morally, intellectually, and physically. Persons have a duty, per this principle, to develop their character in a manner that facilitates moral discernment and steadfastness, while also striving for healthy, well-functioning bodies.

2.8   Case: Cutting Corners

The engineering firm you work for, FreshWater, was the successful bidder for a public–private partnership to build a desalination plant on the California coast. FreshWater won the contract both because it was the lowest bid and because the company has a history of successfully completing similar projects in Saudi Arabia.

You've been appointed as lead engineer for the team responsible for the fluid distribution system and are immediately struck by the small budget allocated for it. You meet with the project manager who tells you, "Oh, don't worry about that. Once you get your plans in place we'll be able to go back and revise upward – this is mainly a government venture, after all!"

Taking her at her word, you devise a complex system in which you rely on high-quality, and more expensive, alloys and seals throughout. You present your completed plans to a meeting with supervising managers from both your company and the state agency. To your surprise, you are chastised for coming in well above budget and told to do a redesign. You meet with the project manager the next day who explains that it is much too late for a total redesign and, by the way, she has already put in the order for the more expensive alloy piping, and hence you'll have to go with much cheaper seals.

In consultation with other team members, you conclude that under most conditions those cheaper seals will be just fine, but should something else fail along the line, they will not likely be able to withstand the higher pressure. Should they fail, the results could be minor (some leaking water) or they could be catastrophic (a total blowout), with, in the worst case, injury or death to any workers in the plant at the time.

You explain all this to the project manager who says that you are overthinking the problem and that there is enough redundancy in the system, so the cheaper seals will be just fine.

What should you do?

NOTES

1. See Chapter 9 for an expansion of this argument.
2. See, for example, Shirley Jackson's short story "The Lottery," first published in 1948.
3. See J.J.C. Smart's similar argument: "For if a case really *did* arise in which injustice was the lesser of two evils, ... then the anti-utilitarian conclusion is a very unpalatable one too, namely that in some circumstances one must choose the greater misery, perhaps the *very much* greater misery, such as that of hundreds of people suffering painful deaths" (Smart and Williams, 1973, 71–72; emphasis original).
4. Some of the text that follows has previously been published in Meyers (2016).
5. This characterization is borrowed from a similar process developed by Dan Wueste (2013).

REFERENCES

Baggini, Julian, and Fosl, Peter S. 2007. *The Ethics Toolkit*. Hoboken, NJ: John Wiley & Sons.

Baggini, Julian, and Fosl, Peter S. 2010. *The Philosopher's Toolkit*, 2nd ed. Hoboken, NJ: John Wiley & Sons.

Beauchamp, Tom, and Childress, James. 1979. *Principles of Biomedical Ethics*. New York: Oxford University Press.

Elliott, Deni, and Ozar, David. 2010. "An Explanation and a Method for Journalism Ethics." In *Journalism Ethics: A Philosophical Approach*, edited by Christopher Meyers, 9–24. New York: Oxford University Press.

Gert, Bernard. 2005. *Morality: Its Nature and Justification*, rev. ed. New York: Oxford University Press.

Hursthouse, Rosalind. 1999. *On Virtue Ethics*. New York: Oxford University Press.

Meyers, Christopher. 2003. "Appreciating W.D. Ross: On Duties and Consequences." *Journal of Mass Media Ethics* 18 (2): 81–97.

Meyers, Christopher. 2011. "Re-appreciating W.D. Ross: Naturalizing Prima Facie Duties and a Proposed Method." *Journal of Mass Media Ethics* 26 (4): 316–331.

Meyers, Christopher. 2016. "Universals without Absolutes: A Theory of Media Ethics." *Journal of Media Ethics* 31 (4): 198–214.

Midgley, Mary. 1981. "Trying Out One's New Sword." In *Heart and Mind*, 69–75. New York: Palgrave Macmillan.

Mill, John Stuart. 1979. *Utilitarianism*, edited by George Sher. Indianapolis: Hackett.

Rawls, John. 1999. *A Theory of Justice*, rev. ed. Cambridge, MA: Belknap Press.

Ross, W.D. (1930) 1988. *The Right and the Good*. Indianapolis, IN: Hackett.

Singer, Peter. 2009. *Animal Liberation: The Definitive Classic of the Animal Movement*, rev. ed. New York: Harper.

Smart, J.J.C., and Williams, Bernard. 1973. *Utilitarianism: For and Against.* Cambridge: Cambridge University Press.

Werhane, Patricia. 1999. *Moral Imagination and Management Decision Making*. New York: Oxford University Press.

Wueste, Dan. 2013. *Ethical Decision Making: A Toolbox Approach*. Clemson, SC: Robert J. Rutland Institute for Ethics.

Part II
Concepts, Principles, and Norms within Professional Environments

Imagine that you are working as a clinical ethics consultant for your local teaching hospital. Given the prominence of the principle of autonomy in health-care ethics, you naturally make it a central element of your teaching and consultations – particularly in the context of the importance of informed consent and end-of-life decision making. Happily, with each such discussion, you get all the right affirmation from the health-care professionals – head nods and verbal commitments to respect and promote patient autonomy. All is good, right?

Well, it would be if everyone involved *meant* the same thing when they invoked the principle. The odds are high, though, that there are at least three different meanings of autonomy at play in such conversations. These range from the Kantian notion that all persons have a unique metaphysical status that demands absolute respect, to the libertarian idea that to be autonomous is just to be a choice maker, to a Millian/Aristotelian developmental view that acting autonomously means pursuing those options that best align with one's life plan.

The Professional Ethics Toolkit, First Edition. Christopher Meyers.
© 2018 John Wiley & Sons Ltd. Published 2018 by John Wiley & Sons Ltd.

The differences are not just semantic. The diverse meanings affect how one understands corresponding ethical duties. Consider informed consent, generally considered to be the paradigm application of autonomy: if different health-care professionals understand its meaning in different ways, this would directly impact on how they would (and should) seek consent. On the Kantian conception, for example, one would recognize a duty to the patient as whole person but may not include the entire decisional context (e.g., family and economics). The libertarian, by comparison, may assume that the patient always knows best and accept every choice, even ill-informed ones, as equally autonomous and valid. Someone with a developmental understanding, on the other hand, would insist that consent processes be richer and more time consuming, with sufficient attention given to understanding the relationship between immediate options and existing or projected life plans.

Some of these differences are rooted in social or institutional cultures, while some come from individuals' education and training. Regardless of the source, the person seeking the best ethical professional choices has to take those histories and contexts into account. For example, say a hospital ethicist believes that autonomy is best understood as a melding of the Kantian and developmental approaches and urges medical staff to approach decisions accordingly. For the harried second-year resident, however, even one who agrees this is what she should be trying to achieve, her world just might not cooperate. Her attending physician may be more sympathetic to a libertarian (any choice is valid) model, layered with a paternalistic beneficence model (putting perceived patient well-being above autonomy). The last thing such an attending physician wants is for the resident to devote her scarcest resource – time – to providing options and discussing risks that may do nothing more than confuse and frighten the patient. In that environment, "informed consent" becomes little more than a form of (perceived) legal self-protection: get the patient to sign the form and make sure that it is placed in the chart.[1]

Now take the complexities and different understandings attached to autonomy and multiply it many times, since, of course, it is but one of a rich set of critical concepts and principles in practical and professional ethics. Those others are similarly subject to varying interpretations and to tensions with other general and role-based duties. It should be obvious, thus, that to fully understand one's ethical principles and duties means to thoroughly understand the underlying concepts, what they *mean* and why they are so *important*.

In this part, the heart of the book, we shall explore several such concepts, ones that regularly pop up in dilemmas and cases. Our strategy will be to engage in conceptual clarification, to try to settle on best definitions, relying on the sort of philosophical evaluation employed in our discussion of the meaning of "professional" in Chapter 1, while also taking into account real-world contingencies. We will also explore why these notions are so important to ethics generally and to professional ethics specifically, while also considering how they manifest across a range of professions and contexts and situating them within common ethics cases. In alphabetical order, we shall explore autonomy and respect, beneficence and non-maleficence, competency, confidentiality, conflict of interest, fidelity, honesty and role-based duties, and justice, both formal and distributive.

NOTE

1. Such an approach does not, in fact, serve to legally immunize one. Should litigation ensue, the whole consent process will be evaluated, with the signed form commonly treated as largely irrelevant to whether the patient in fact provided consent.

3 Autonomy and Respect for Persons

3.1	Autonomy in the World	75
3.2	The Hard Work of Being Autonomous	82
3.3	Case: Which Autonomous Voice?	86
	Notes	88
	References	88

"A little professionalism, people. When asking a patient to undress, we do not giggle."

Autonomy and respect are among the most important moral concepts in professional ethics – maybe *the* most important – with deep sources in both theoretical and practical ethics. While arguably less valued in Eastern cultures, they are typically cited as the central principle in Western practical ethics interactions. For example, Charles Fried describes their importance in the physician–client relationship by noting, "The doctor's prime and basic function is … the preservation of life capacities for the realization of a reasonable, realistic life plan … the doctor must see himself as the servant, not of life in the abstract, but of life plans of his patients" (1974, 98).

And, importantly, the principles demand not just that we honor the moral status of *clients* but also that of *professionals*. Among the more challenging professional ethics issues, for example, are cases in which the professional's autonomy is in conflict with the client's or with an important social good. Consider, for example, some health-care professionals' desire not to have to participate in health practices – typically reproductive or end-of-life practices – that they see as violating their morality.

As we saw in Chapter 2, however, the meaning of autonomy (and, to a lesser extent, of respect) varies considerably, which certainly makes prioritizing it difficult. If we do not agree on what it means, how do we make sure that it is always respected and promoted?

The version I commend here has become dominant among practicing and academic ethicists in that it both borrows from theoretical foundations and takes into account what it means to be an autonomous agent in the real world. I will explain each element in fuller detail in due course, but for now here is a working characterization:

- Autonomy *means* making choices within the context of genuine options, while not being overly coerced or constrained, having access to relevant information and the ability to understand it, and using that information to make choices that best align with one's life plan.
- Autonomy is *valuable* because it is the foundation of morality. We respect persons as carrying the highest moral worth because they are capable of being moral agents, of making choices, and of

being held responsible for them. Autonomy makes such choices possible, through which, persons are able to fulfill their greatest potential. As we discussed in Chapter 2, respect for persons is among the most stringent of moral principles, bordering on being an absolute dictum. Its corollary, autonomy, however, carries lower moral weight. As we shall see, it routinely conflicts with other moral goods – including others' autonomy – and thus is subject to the same reasoned balancing as pertains to the other principles.

- Autonomy is *achieved* through an array of social, professional, and institutional mechanisms, including education, respecting rights, and effective communication, especially when a more knowledgeable person is assisting another in making important choices.

I shall spell out the sources of this characterization shortly. For now, consider the following scenario as it elucidates the concept in practice.

─────────── 3.1 Autonomy in the World ───────────

Picture the following scenario. A husband and wife have regretfully decided to end their marriage. They still care for each other but are moving in different directions. They have not lived together for a few months and she lets him know that she is now dating someone else and has been since they first separated.

Thankfully there are no children, but they do have a fairly sizable estate that both worked hard to build. He recognizes, though, that his profession gives him greater lifetime earning power and offers a 60/40 split (in her favor), which she gratefully accepts.

Both have hired lawyers to make sure all the *t*'s are crossed and *i*'s dotted. When the husband explains the proposed property arrangement to his lawyer, she explodes: "You did what?! Right now, your wife's attorney is no doubt telling her she can get even more, so we have to start building our case." He is taken aback, but decides to hear her out, during which he casually notes his wife's new relationship. The lawyer about jumps out of her chair: "We have her! This isn't a no-fault state – if she's been shacking up with someone else, we can get at least 75 percent of the assets." He balks, but she continues to press. By the end of the meeting, she has convinced him that he deserves the money, that if he doesn't attack they will take him for even more, and that his wife's new relationship is a terrible betrayal.

Sure enough, the husband's lawyer successfully negotiates for 75 percent and they all meet to sign the final paperwork and get the judge's approval. He drives there in good spirits but, as soon as he sees his soon to be ex-wife, he feels a pang of remorse. He suppresses it but later realizes, after all is said and done, that he never once looked her in the eye.

Setting aside whether the case's outcome was ethically optimal,[1] the question for the moment is whether the process respected the husband's autonomy. On the surface, it certainly appears that it did. He's a smart guy, he understood all the goings on, he explicitly agreed to this strategy, and there was no undue coercion. In order to effectively judge whether that first take is sufficient, however, let us first consider some other autonomy-related ethical issues.

Gravely ill children who have not responded to standard treatment protocols are sometimes presented with the option of participating in what is called a phase 1 clinical trial. In such experiments there is no expectation that the proposed drug will benefit the child – it may, but there is no reason to think that it will. Instead, the goal is to determine whether the drug is safe, what the best dosage levels are, and if there are negative side effects. The children are often as young as three, so informed consent must be obtained from the parents or guardian. If they agree to proceed, however, in most cases the child still has the right to refuse. The thinking is that only the adults can understand well enough whether the child should participate in the trial but that the child knows enough to say "no" (e.g., out of fear of pain or other discomfort).[2] In the literature, the distinction is typically characterized as "consent" (what an adult can give) and "assent" (a child's right of refusal).

In contrast, children are not typically given the right to refuse clearly beneficial interventions, even ones with negative side effects. The best-known example is that of children of Jehovah's Witness parents. While adult adherents can, and typically do, refuse blood products for themselves (they interpret a passage in the Bible as prohibiting its "ingestion"), most states do not give them that right when it comes to their children. Nor do they let the child refuse, believing that she or he does not yet have enough life experience, that is, a sufficiently developed life plan, to make such a critical choice. At the same time, however, many judges will allow a "mature minor" refusal rights (such minors are typically aged fifteen or older and are fairly sophisticated in their reasoning and understanding).

At first glance, this all seems like a muddled mess, especially for those who want a clean, binary definition of key concepts like autonomy, who seek the neatness of "either you are autonomous or you are not." But all the scenarios certainly share something in common: All involve *choices* and thus, per our working characterization, all thereby involve autonomy, at least in *some* fashion. But they are also very different kinds of choices, with widely different levels of understanding, external constraints, external and internal coercion, and background experience. So, if autonomy is at work in each, it surely is to *variable degrees*. That conclusion presumes, thus, that the concept of autonomy admits of degrees, that some choices are more or less autonomous than others. That may sound plausible, and it is at least implied in our characterization, but you should know that it runs contrary to one of the better-known and more highly respected analyses of the concept – Immanuel Kant's.

3.1.1 Kant and moral agency

Kant's approach is central to much of ethics theory while also informing key elements of practical and professional ethics, and with good reason. It is sophisticated and connects with our core intuitions about how we should relate with one another morally. For Kant, as revealed in his comments about persons' *noumenal* nature, autonomy connects to a *status*; it is the metaphysical *capacity* that makes freedom and moral accountability possible and is thereby also the grounding for the powerful modern notion of human dignity or respect, with the corresponding attachment of *natural rights*.

Briefly reiterating our discussion from Chapter 2, Kant was deeply struck by humans' capacity for reasoning and, seemingly, genuinely free choice. Our bodies, however, are strictly material and are thus subject to natural laws of cause and effect (thereby precluding original free agency). Yet, he says, we also have direct *experience* of free choices. The only explanation, he concluded, is that humans must also have a non-material nature, a nature not subject to physical cause and effect and thus capable of free choice. Most importantly, that capacity for autonomous free choice is also what allows persons to be justly held morally accountable and thus to be afforded such profound moral respect; it is what makes persons *moral agents*.

Think of it this way: if a rock rolls down a hill and crushes some poor soul who happens to be walking by, we do not chastise the rock ("Bad rock! Don't you *ever* do that again"). The rock, after all, made no choice – it does not have choice-making capacities. It was just dumb luck that erosion and gravity came together at the wrong time. But, if some person is at the top of the hill, lying in wait for the passer-by, and *pushes* the rock with the intent of crushing the passer-by, we would very likely hold that person accountable for his murderous choice. Why? Because, per Kant, he has an autonomous will that allows him to *choose* whether to act on his evil impulses.

He also has reasoning capabilities that allow him to understand the facts of the matter – big, hard rock versus small, soft body – and to recognize the logical implications of his actions. By contrast, if a three-year-old loosed the (obviously already precarious) rock, we would not hold her accountable, since children are not capable of such understanding or reasoning: she did not – *could* not – know that pushing on the rock would produce such tragic consequences. Nor do we (properly) hold animals morally accountable; a horse could not know, for example, that kicking the rock would result in another's death.[3]

Kant's full vision is much more complicated, with notoriously difficult arguments about the relationship between reason, morality, and genuine autonomy. Recall, however, our discussion in Chapter 2 about the relatively straightforward and intuitively powerful notion that there is something morally special about persons: they should not be used as mere means – that is, as tools or objects – in the satisfaction of others' desires. In language more prevalent in professional ethics, persons must be *respected* – as whole persons, not just, say, as a kidney that needs repair. Such respect also imposes, for example, the requirement that one has a right to legal representation when one is accused of a crime, and that a professor may not harass her students.

While many scholars and ethicists reject Kant's entire metaphysics,[4] his emphasis on respect for persons and its essential connection to autonomy still pervades the literature, as does his discussion of the role of understanding and rationality in determinations of moral accountability.

3.1.2 Mill and developed selfhood

Understanding and rationality are also foundational to a Millian understanding of autonomy, which he takes to be rooted in the *development of selfhood*. Much of *On Liberty* (Mill, 1956) is devoted to discussing the conditions that contribute to selfhood, to what he considers to be fully realized individuality. Persons with such individuality possess, in his terms, advanced "human faculties of perception, judgment, discriminative feeling, mental activity, and even moral preference" (Mill, 1956, 71).

On his model, clearly Aristotelian in origin, much of life is spent becoming more autonomous – wiser, more discerning, and better able to reason. Unlike for Kant, however, autonomy is not valuable in itself; rather, it is a tool for helping persons to achieve as much happiness (very richly understood) as possible, for themselves and, true to his utilitarian theory, for society. Only through its implementation can persons come to better recognize what is truly important to them, individually and collectively.

Such autonomous individuality is achievable solely through education and experience; thus, Mill says, individuality can be present, and thus must be respected, only when education and experience – especially education – are sufficiently present. For example, in one of his more infamous passages he states that "despotism is a legitimate mode of government in dealing with barbarians," given their uneducated, "backward" condition (Mill, 1956, 14). He further notes that it is proper to restrain someone when they are ignorant about an impending threat (Mill, 1956, 117), and even that education should be compulsory (Mill, 1956, 128). Doing so enriches their self-understanding and allows them, again, to make choices that are more likely to contribute to their own and to the aggregate good.

Contrary, thus, to his reputation as a libertarian, these passages show that Mill would in fact reject that simplistic characterization of autonomy (to be autonomous is to make choices). Instead, he insists that only through education and experience can one make the choices that will enhance happiness.

3.1.3   Variable autonomy, life plans, and identity

All of this should answer the earlier question about whether autonomy admits of degrees. Each of its core elements – understood in shorthand as *respect, free choice*, and *selfhood* – clearly have variable quality. The latter two are straightforward. First, all human choice is subject to varying degrees of coercion and constraint, both external (e.g., power and economic pressure) and internal (e.g., fear and insecurity). Second, one's selfhood, one's sense of *identity*, is enriched, becomes fuller, as one moves through life, gaining experience and becoming more educated. Through this, persons also come to define who they are; they develop and seek to promote a *life plan*. As a child, or even an inexperienced or uneducated young adult, one generally cannot be expected to have a coherent vision of where one fits into the world, who one wants to be, and where one wants to end up. One's identity is not yet (fully) formed. Thus, the more experience one gains, the more education one acquires, and the more autonomous one is the better one will be at making choices that align with that identity.

Even *respect*, now that it is divorced from Kant's problematic metaphysics, admits of degrees. One can, for example, fully respect an adult human, embracing thereby her status as a person with dignity and in possession of the full complement of human rights. At the same time, one can similarly conclude that, say, a dog should be afforded *some* level of respect – including a recognition of (lesser) dignity and (fewer) rights, such as, at the very least, the right not to be caused to suffer needlessly.

Similarly, if also more problematic: should an adult human suffer trauma that puts him in a permanent vegetative state, the moral requirements of dignity and respect also shift. For example, while he is healthy, we are clearly obligated to provide him with minimal life-saving medical interventions. In his now devastated and irrecoverable condition, however, as the courts and the ethics literature have consistently determined, such medical intervention is neither legally nor ethically mandatory. Put differently: If one were forced to choose between this person's earlier healthy and his now ravaged "self," surely our greater duty is to the former. Parallel analyses can be provided along the spectrum of autonomous selfhood: the great apes should be afforded greater respect than squirrels, as should cetaceans over sea slugs.

3.1.4   Contributing and detracting factors

As these examples suggest, there are any number of factors that serve to enhance and to damage persons' autonomous development. Among the enhancing factors are social connections, educational opportunities, economic security, and skillful communication, particularly from the professional to the client. Among those that damage are the reverse of those (i.e., social isolation, educational ignorance, poverty, and inferior communication) but also fear, arrogance, pain, power differential, and time constraints. All of these make it harder – in some cases impossible – for persons to make choices consistent with their life plans.

These discussions undoubtedly raise as many questions as they answer, some extraordinarily difficult and beyond the scope of this exploration. For example, how should we weigh respect – particularly if that is translated into the provision of scarce resources – for a severely disabled infant who will never develop and will probably survive at most several days, against, say, the ongoing obliteration of African elephants? There are also obvious implications for the abortion and assisted suicide and euthanasia debates.

─────── 3.2   The Hard Work of Being Autonomous ───────

Consider again the skills and character traits Mill describes (in section 3.1.2) as being possessed by the autonomous individual: advanced "human faculties of perception, judgment, discriminative feeling, mental activity, and even moral preference." None of these just springs into existence: There is *hard work* involved in their development and sustainment. In Aristotelian language, autonomous decision-making is an acquired *skill*, part of the development of practical wisdom and emerging from habituated dedication (Meyers, 2004).[5] It also demands diligence and courage, that is, a willingness to take the risks associated with questioning the status quo. But if one requirement of ethics reasoning is, per Step 2 in our guide, sometimes to have to step outside the box to achieve creative, morally imaginative solutions, such risk taking is unavoidable.

Because such development, by definition, occurs incrementally, we again see that autonomy admits of degrees. The practical import of this is apparent when, as in the examples cited earlier, considering whether to give mature children or young adults the right to make their own decisions. The more developed their "human faculties" are the more comfortable others can feel about allowing them to make major, even potentially life-changing, decisions – which is, of course, exactly the sort of evaluation judges undertake when deciding whether an adolescent meets "mature minor" criteria. Among the key concerns is how much opportunity they have had to exercise their reasoning skills, as opposed to being under an authoritative family or religious figure who discouraged or even forbade such independence. One must also take into account what is at stake – children are rightly given the choice whether, say, to eat the hospital food; at what age, though, should they be allowed to choose whether to do a two-day liquid fast? We have devised ultimately arbitrary criteria for certain choices: One must be 18 years old to vote, but not 17 years and 364 days; 21 to drink; but 18 to smoke. Assessing someone's reasoning skills would certainly be more rational, but it is not feasible on a large scale.

More controversial is whether and how to assess reasoning levels in *adults*, particularly when those choices also conflict with other persons' rights or with important social goods. The United States has long insisted that persons who wish to be exempted from military service – so-called conscientious objectors – be able to provide strong evidence of a rich, consistent, and well-developed belief system for such exemptions to be granted. Should similar standards be applied in other areas, for example when professionals seek exemption from standard professional practice?

It is, of course, important to respect professionals' autonomy in the same ways as we do clients'; they too wish to develop and fulfill life plans and to be rightly held accountable for their choices. In recognition of these values, most states have legislation that allows health-care professionals to be excused from participating in certain health-care services, typically those related to reproductive or end-of-life care. But most also require nothing in the way of justification: California's example is typical in that it merely demands that the professional sign a declaration indicating that she has a "moral, ethical, or religious objection" to participating in the service (Meyers and Woods, 1996). Given that there are serious rights questions at stake, rights comparable to the social goods present in the military exemption case, the question is whether such professionals should also have to provide evidence of sophisticated reasoning.

As you can imagine, any such suggestion is highly controversial (Card, 2007), with reactions ranging from knee-jerk and overly facile references to the First Amendment's liberty protections, to equally knee-jerk and facile claims of "you knew what you were getting into." Those who would demand that the exemption-seeking professional provide developed reasons are thereby stating that one must be able to exercise – and *reveal* – the kind of insight, judgment, and discrimination that Mill describes, at least on matters that significantly impact others; otherwise, such choices may be overridden. But what counts as sufficiently sophisticated and who will make that determination? And, just as with children, the level of sophistication surely must vary according to the importance of the decision, making a complicated issue nearly impenetrable.

These sorts of autonomy-driven dilemmas suggest two conclusions. First, autonomy is among the more important of moral principles in practical and professional ethics, so important that we have to work hard to understand its meaning and value, in all their complexity; second, the kinds of dilemmas that emerge from those analyses are, to reinforce a key theme of this book, *very hard* to work through. Hence, circling back to the opening of this section, one can appreciate the temptation to just fall back on a simplistic, binary characterization of autonomy, of the sort captured in the libertarian view. Doing so, however, simplifies only temporarily, as the harder questions have a way of reasserting themselves eventually, typically in ways that are even more complex and difficult to resolve.

3.2.1   Additional examples

Most of the examples of this point have been rooted in health care, but autonomy is of course deeply present in all the professions. As noted in the Introduction, having autonomous control over one's practice is one of the central features of a profession, any profession. Further, among the most important of professional activities is assisting clients in achieving their autonomous life plans. Further examples, thus, of autonomy's role across the professions include the following;

- How much latitude should college students be given in choosing their course of study? Should faculty impose strict general education requirements, or allow, even encourage, students to pursue their own interests outside the major? Similarly, how much control should administrators or other professors impose on faculty regarding course content or structure?
- Most engineers work for firms that have well-established processes and protocols for how to design and complete projects. Is there room within that setting for individual engineers to express autonomous control over non-safety questions? Even more significantly, at what point should an engineer's autonomous judgment about a safety or quality question justify reporting concerns to outside regulators (Weil, 2006)?
- Should an architect attempt to override a client who, in the architect's professional judgment, is insisting on a home design that is unnecessarily expensive, unattractive, a nuisance for neighbors, or environmentally unsound (Khederian, 2012)? Or, similarly, when should a Certified Public Accountant (CPA) refuse to support a client's overly risky investment plans?
- One of the most difficult tasks veterinarians routinely face is euthanizing pets. Should they participate in such an act if they believe that the client is doing it for mere convenience reasons? How should they go about assessing the client's reasons?
- When, if ever, should attorneys pressure a client into a different legal strategy than the one the client initially presented?

The last example takes us back to the scenario with which we opened this chapter. Given what we now know about autonomy – that it admits of degrees and that the most autonomous choices are those that align with persons' deepest values and life plans – we see why it makes sense to question whether the husband's lawyer respected and promoted his autonomy. We obviously have limited facts here but, based on the available information, I would say that she did not. He obviously made a choice – a rational choice and one not overly coerced or constrained. But, given the values reflected in his initial decision about how to split the property, given the power asymmetry present in the relationship with the attorney and the associated alienation he felt in the situation, given the apparent remorse he experienced, and given the ruin of any remaining relationship with his former spouse, the evidence suggests that his choices were not in fact fully autonomous: they did not align with his developed life plan.

This is not to say that those choices were wholly *heteronomous*: he is not our unthinking rock. His overall status as someone capable of developed autonomy, even if those capabilities were not fully expressed in this case, further show that one would be hard pressed to suggest that some wiser soul should have come into the picture and coerced the husband into making a different choice (though one might wish that a judge would explore more deeply what the parties genuinely hoped to achieve). The question here is whether the *attorney* thoroughly respected and promoted her client's autonomy: did she fulfill her professional obligation to help him achieve his developed life plan? Per the argument above, it would appear not.

These discussions also explain the thinking behind the distinction between "assent" and "consent." The former does not assume developed autonomy, while the latter does, at least to a significant extent. We also see now why judges have consistently ruled that young children cannot make life-and-death choices such as whether to refuse life-saving blood products; they just have not yet lived enough to be able to make choices that, in essence, preclude any other life plan. And, yet, those same judges might conclude that an older, much more mature adolescent has lived enough life to wholly orient his life plan around his now sufficiently developed faith.

Let us close with a case that asks you to analyze your understanding of autonomy and to exercise ethics reasoning.

———— 3.3   Case: Which Autonomous Voice? ————

Mr. Smith has been diagnosed with delusional dementia and has been a patient in a long-term mental health facility for some ten years. Prior to his illness, he had been a respected college professor, known for his rich grasp of historical details and insightful analyses of world events. His current cognitive status is episodic. He will have periods of pretty sharp lucidity but then fall back into severe delusions. He seems, though, to be quite happy in those latter states; the most common version of late is his belief that he is a Norse god with a range of supernatural powers (that he cannot effectuate those powers does not seem to bother him in the least).

The ratio of lucid to delusional has significantly worsened over the last year; he is now delusional nearly all the time, with only occasional periods of clear thinking. He has no family and no written advance directive. Other than intermittent urinary tract infections (UTIs) secondary to incontinence, his physical health is quite good; he could easily live another twenty years. His mental problems, however, have proven resistant to all forms of therapeutic intervention. It looks like he will soon be permanently delusional.

During his most recent period of clarity, he insisted that he did not want to live like this. He has no memories from his delusional states; as far as he can tell, he is unconscious for increasingly longer periods of time, with confusion and disorientation as to what has transpired during the interim.

He reassures his treating team that he is not asking them to actively end his life; rather, he just requests that the next UTI go untreated, allowing sepsis to set in, followed by a relatively pain-free death. The psychiatrist in charge of his case struggles over the request, but after discussing it with the rest of the treating team and further with the patient, she agrees.

Some six months later the patient acquires another UTI while in his delusional state. Feeling the discomfort and growing lethargy, he asks for treatment. Not knowing how to respond, the nurse calls for the psychiatrist, who explains to the patient the agreement they had reached earlier. The patient vociferously objects: "*I* did not reach that agreement with you. I want to live! You have to treat me!!"

Assume that the psychiatrist is committed to protecting and promoting the patient's autonomy: What should she do? Which choice is the (most) autonomous? Can both choices be equally autonomous and, if so, which should she respect? Should she simply ignore the autonomy question and base her choice on some other moral principle(s)?

NOTES

1. Nothing in the process or outcome even bordered on illegality and the lawyer's actions were wholly consistent with legal ethics standards.
2. Part of my training included a rotation at St. Jude Children's Hospital, a setting in which these choices were all too frequent. According to the health-care professionals, very few children in fact refused. Some clearly were trying to please their parents – who were sometimes grasping at any hope of successful intervention – but some also explicitly said, "If it can help some other child, I'll do it." They showed, in other words, bravery well beyond that of many adults.
3. Persons, of course, rightly use negative reinforcement to *train* animals, but *punishing* them – possibly excepting other high-level mammals, for example, great apes – for their behavior is both nonsensical and cruel. Consider the infamous case of Big Mary, the elephant hanged for killing her handler in 1916 in Kingsport, Tennessee (http://www.nydailynews. com/news/national/fed-circus-elephant-lynched-murder-1916-article-1.2149605, accessed August 22, 2017).
4. Of the many contentious elements of Kant's metaphysics, one that is particularly relevant to practical and professional ethics is that, on a strict reading, he would not count very young children as moral agents with associated rights to life and liberty (Tooley, 1972), let alone very sophisticated non-human mammals (http://www.nonhumanrightsproject.org) or, potentially, advanced artificial intelligence (Barrat, 2015).
5. Kant makes a similar argument in his discussion of "enlightenment," a status very similar to that of Mill's developed individual: "If I have a book to serve as my understanding, a pastor to serve as my conscience, a physician to determine my diet," I will never reach my greatest intellectual and moral potential" (Kant, 1983, 41).

REFERENCES

Barrat, James. 2015. *Our Final Invention: Artificial Intelligence and the End of the Human Era*. New York: St. Martin's Griffin.
Card, Robert F. 2007. "Conscientious Objection and Emergency Contraception." *American Journal of Bioethics* 7 (6): 8–14.
Fried, Charles. 1974. *Medical Experimentation: Personal Integrity and Social Policy*. New York: Elsevier.

Kant, Immanuel. 1983. "An Answer to the Question: What Is Enlightenment?" In *Perpetual Peace and Other Essays*, translated and with an introduction by Ted Humphrey, 41–48. Indianapolis: Hackett.

Khederian, Robert. 2012. "The 10 Ugliest McMansions in New Jersey." http://www.complex.com/style/2012/07/the-10-ugliest-mcmansions-in-new-jersey, accessed August 22, 2017.

Meyers, Christopher. 2004. "Cruel Choices: Autonomy and Critical Care Decision-Making." *Bioethics* 18 (2): 104–119.

Meyers, Christopher, and Woods, Robert. 1996. "An Obligation to Provide Abortion Services: What Happens When Physicians Refuse?" *Journal of Medical Ethics* 22 (2): 115–120.

Mill, John Stuart. 1956. *On Liberty*, edited and with an introduction by C.V. Shields. Indianapolis: Library of Liberal Arts.

Tooley, Michael. 1972. "Abortion and Infanticide," *Philosophy & Public Affairs*, 2 (1): 37–65.

Weil, Vivian. 2006. "Whistleblowing: What Have We Learned Since the Challenger?" National Society of Professional Engineers. http://www.nspe.org/resources/ethics/ethics-resources/other-resources/whistleblowing-what-have-we-learned-challenger, accessed August 22, 2017.

4 Beneficence and Non-Maleficence

4.1	Beneficence	93
4.2	Non-Maleficence	97
4.3	Cases	100
	Notes	102
	References	103

" I thought you were supposed to do no harm ! "

"First, and above all else, do no harm [*primum non nocere*]" has long been considered to be the most basic of moral dictates for medicine,[1] but any profession would do well to recognize the core intuitive power of the principle of non-maleficence. As discussed in Chapter 2, every system of ethics embraces the idea that it is wrong to cause others avoidable harm. Combine this with the role of professionals in helping manage *vital interests*, with the associated potential for great harm, and non-maleficence emerges as a core moral guidepost.

Non-maleficence is, in fact, for many *the* most stringent principle. Kant, for example, considered non-maleficence a "perfect" duty, one that it is always wrong to violate, while beneficence was an imperfect duty, good to follow, but with a range of valid exceptions. That value ranking is also broadly present in Western political foundations, revealed for example in the fact that nearly all the enumerated rights in the US Constitution are meant to protect against infringement, as opposed to requiring persons to assist others.

The highly respected contemporary utilitarian, Peter Singer, has committed much of his work to challenging this ranking, reminding us, through simple thought experiments, that sometimes a duty to help is as compelling as one not to hurt. Among his most persuasive is the following scenario. Imagine you are walking along and notice that a child has fallen face first into a shallow pool of water. No one else is nearby and you quickly realize that if you do nothing the child will drown. You also realize that you can save her quite easily, with little more than inconvenience to yourself. Should you wade in and grab her? (Singer, 1997).[2]

I have presented this question to at least a thousand people, of all ages and from all backgrounds, and have *never* had someone seriously suggest that one does not have a strict duty to assist her; everyone recognizes that not doing so is plainly unethical. (Or at least they do this after being given assurances of their own safety – it is not a raging river – and that they are protected under a Good Samaritan law – the rescuer is immune from litigation for all but gross negligence.)

This consistent result is striking for at least a couple of reasons. First, this level of unanimity on moral concerns is highly unusual, as is the consensus on the supporting reason, that a child's life is of great moral value, certainly far greater than any inconvenience caused in saving her. The recognition of such value is further expressed when the scenario is progressively altered to raise the stakes: you are wearing your brand new and expensive Italian loafers; you are already running a bit late to a job interview at your dream workplace; the water is deep enough that you might have to swim a bit. Again, the near-universal reaction is that a child's life is worth more than a pair of shoes, or a job, or some physical exertion. The commitment to help is typically sustained until there is some genuine threat to the rescuer (e.g., there are crocodiles in the water), though even here most think that we have a strong duty at least to *try*.

Second, and more pertinent to our immediate purpose, the scenario reveals that we have *positive duties to help others* (beneficence), not just negative ones not to cause harm (non-maleficence). The rescuer has done nothing to contribute to the child's predicament; he just happens to stumble onto the scene. And yet he has a *strict* duty to assist, to benefit someone else in need. In fact, most people conclude that there is no moral difference between someone merely standing there, gleefully watching the child drown and having pushed her in; both are clearly and equally unethical. For Singer and others,[3] these "intuition pumps" reveal that, despite many persons' initial impressions, beneficence is as compelling a moral duty as non-maleficence.

We need not resolve this debate here. My anecdotal survey is hardly definitive – every one of the thousand people could well be mistaken – and any number of theorists have questioned just how much we can conclude from Singer's example. For our purposes, we need only recognize that beneficence has a *powerful* moral standing – particularly so for the professions, whose very purpose is to help persons in need. This recognition is what, in fact, drives many of those who go into the professions. Lives are lived better and more richly through positive service to others, especially when compared to a life spent merely not causing harm or, worse, devoting a life to singularly self-interested pursuit of profit and material goods (Brooks, 2015).

In this chapter we shall first explore the meaning and value of beneficence, giving particular attention to the complexities involved in its real-world use. We shall then do the same with non-maleficence, before closing with cases that will challenge you to determine their best practical application, particularly in balance with one another and with other principles.

4.1 Beneficence

Recall our definition from Chapter 2: "Persons should do what they reasonably can to improve the situation of others" – not just avoid causing harm, but actively seek to assist others in need, including doing what one can to *protect* others from threats.

Beneficence, thus, is at the very heart of professionalism. To be a professional is, we have learned, to be "an expert skilled in the provision of vital services, who has a normative commitment to their clients' well-being." Beneficence is embedded in that definition in two key ways. First, the services are vital because there is much at stake for the client – he has real needs – and the skilled expert can effectively help in their resolution. And, second, being a professional includes the now familiar emphasis on prioritizing the client's well-being. Beneficence is also present in the duty to be available twenty-four hours a day, seven days a week – a generous commitment to help others at all hours of the day and night.

Simple enough, right? All of us, and professionals especially, should do what we reasonably can to improve the lives of others. The difficulty lies in *balance*: How much beneficence do we owe others and at what costs? When does enough become too much, such that there is a diminishing return? And are persons able to make that call *objectively*? Even if we can accurately answer these questions, what level of sacrifice is realistic to expect of persons, given human nature?

At various stages of his career Singer has urged quite extensive philanthropy, including in a 2006 interview, in which he suggests that New Yorkers could reasonably live on only 10 percent of their discretionary income (Singer, 2006). Those of us who live comfortably in wealthy nations, have a duty to give *a lot*, essentially everything beyond what is needed to be able to live comfortably. We cannot, he says, justify purchasing relative luxuries while others starve. And, just as controversially, he has long argued that our duties are as great to strangers on the other side of the planet as they are to those close to us.

He has recently tempered both positions and now says that we should give at least 1 percent of our annual income to worldwide relief organizations (Singer, 2010), while also recognizing that societies are made better (i.e., there is more utilitarian benefit) when we commit ourselves first to caring for those closest to us. Other approaches view it as more like the role of progressive tax models in systems of distributive justice (see Chapter 9). Those who have the most should give the most – not just in absolute dollars but also proportionally, considering the luxurious lives the wealthiest enjoy.

4.1.1   Finding balance in the professions

For professionals, the determination of how much is enough is typically translated into the giving of *time* and *expertise*, rather than (or in addition to) monetary donations. And, while there is a generalized duty for all professionals to assist with vital needs, this has to be balanced against the particular duty to assist one's primary clients. As beneficent as it might be to provide career counseling or philosophical elucidation to any person who comes in off the street, clearly I have a greater duty to prioritize the students I am currently teaching and advisees whom I have explicitly taken on.

While assistance to primary clients has, in most circumstances, first priority, the more generalized professional duty to be available at all hours to *all* those in need is sharply revealed in times of emergency, when professionals must be willing to provide needed services, even potentially at the sacrifice of their own well-being. Consider, for example, the public health professionals' commitment to report for duty during a "medical surge" (e.g., a natural disaster or terrorist attack), even if they have not been able to confirm the safety of family members. How much one is needed in such situations is obviously profession dependent: engineers will likely be in far greater demand than architects, as would clinical ethicists than philosophy professors. That difference, though, is not driven by a lesser obligation of beneficence but rather by the relative expertise and associated needs; further, keep in mind that any professional can fulfill her duty through broader service (e.g., helping to distribute food and water or to sanitize hospital settings).

Nearly all professionals lament just how difficult it is to balance even routine demands to help others. Physicians and lawyers, for example, often describe requests for their time as potentially limitless. And, even in less front-line professions, the workload can appear unrelenting. One could, for example, commit endless time to prepping for a class and faculty routinely just have to declare, "This is good enough." Beyond some basic triage, how does one balance those competing needs, let alone also find time for family or personal growth?

And, just to make it even more complicated, there are legitimate concerns about whether beneficent help may harm more than it aids, for example by causing recipients to be dependent on that assistance or by making them feel inferior to those giving it (Lupton, 2011). Note, however, that none of these problems get at the core claim that we have a strong duty to help others; rather, they just reveal that determining the proper balance is tremendously difficult and riddled with empirical and psychological problems.

It should be obvious that attempts to promote beneficence also routinely run up against other moral duties. For example, should society focus more on beneficent rehabilitation or formal, especially retributive, justice? Is it acceptable to tell a white lie to make someone happy? What about coercing a decision that one believes is in someone's best interest, even if they say that they want something to the contrary?

4.1.2   Paternalistic beneficence?

That last question has long been particularly vexing for professionals. Is it better to be paternalistically beneficent or to respect clients' autonomous, if also sometimes imprudent, choices? Paternalism certainly dominated through the mid-1970s, with the thinking being that the professional was the expert and knew better than the client what was in his best interest. Toward the end of that decade and concurrent with the "democratization" of the professions (indeed, of society generally: see Epilogue), professional ethics took a sharp turn toward granting clients greater decision-making authority. In part as a response to concerns about coerced medical experimentation (US Department of Health and Human Services, 1979), autonomy became, as we saw in Chapter 3, dominant, serving as the strongest underpinning of emerging models of professional ethics (Beauchamp and Childress, 1977; Veatch, 1981).

That break from paternalism was certainly in large part justified. Professionals too frequently made value-driven decisions that aligned with *their* ethical norms, not necessarily those of their clients, including norms driven by professional cultures: if you are a hammer (or a surgeon or lawyer), everything looks like a nail (or something to cut with or to argue about). The whole point of the "client-centered" movement is that even minor variations in values or life plans can make major differences in how best to resolve problems. The finest professionals have always found a way to communicate effectively with clients, seeking to discover *their* wishes, to create a genuine decision-making partnership. But, realistically, most professionals simply told clients what to do and the client went along with it.

That paternalistic model started to break down when a confluence of factors – for example, professional services increasingly being seen as a money-making opportunity and society generally shifting power away from the elite and toward the citizenry – came together in the mid- to late-1970s. Client autonomy became the mantra, but too often with an overly simplistic understanding of that principle. Even early on, ethicists began to see how that simplicity created a whole new set of problems (Ackerman, 1982). Further, anyone working in professional settings knows that an altered form of paternalism is still pervasive. Clients are typically given a single option to which they invariably agree, with the pretense of genuine consent nominally reified on a form. That is, in most decisions, clients merely *assent* to the professional's recommendation; they do not genuinely *consent*, in accordance with their life plan.

Proponents of the autonomy turn decry this reality and there is no question that the best professional ethics strive for a genuine partnership in which the client explains his values and goals and the professional uses her expertise to try to effectuate them, within the constraints extant in the presenting problem and consistent with best professional practice. And remember that those constraints can be overwhelming, even to the most assertive individual (see the range of factors discussed in Chapter 3 that constrain one's ability to make choices consistent with developed autonomy).

While the professions should assuredly be striving to eradicate some of those constraints (abuse of power asymmetry, arrogance, conflicting financial incentives, dual obligations), others are structurally embedded in the very reasons that persons seek professional help in the first place (fear, pain, alienation, ignorance). And, as so embedded, the soundest ethical response will often, in fact, be a form of beneficent paternalism (Schneider, 1998; Zacharias, 2001).

In short, a facile view of autonomy decries any paternalistic intervention, no matter how well intentioned. But, as we've already seen, autonomy, important as it is, has to be weighed against other compelling principles, especially beneficence, and to be viewed within the real-world context that constrains developed autonomous choices. The ethically committed professional recognizes that each situation and each person brings different factors to the table and undertakes the careful ethics reasoning needed to achieve the best balance.

4.2   Non-Maleficence

Given the complexities inherent in striving to promote beneficence, you can no doubt appreciate the temptation to make it all simpler, or seemingly simpler, by just focusing on not harming others. While that might work in strictly instrumental relationships – "Yes, I cannot defraud you while selling you a car, but I don't have to help you out by getting you a great deal" – professional relationships are structurally different: the very *purpose* of the interaction is to help someone in need.

What then do we make of the perceived primary status of *primum non nocere?* In simple terms, the dictate demands that professionals *not make things worse.* Strive to help, for sure, but also make sure you do not bungle so badly that your clients are worse off because of your "assistance."

Part of the urgency of this demand exists in the realization that professionals routinely and unavoidably cause significant harm in the course of achieving the intended good. Harm is, in fact, an essential element of many professional activities: surgeons cannot heal without also bringing about physical injury; lawyers routinely have to cut deals that leave their clients better off in the long run but cause real harm up front (jail time, financial settlement); physicians regularly prescribe medicine that damages some cells while repairing others; and professors harm their students through the stress and anxiety attached to exams, papers, and grades.

For harm to be justified, it must be outweighed by competing moral goods – beneficence, typically, but also autonomy, justice, and dignity. And the justification, of course, assumes that the good outcome actually comes to pass; if not, the professional has only harmed the client or, at best, left him no better and no worse off (but nearly always assuredly *poorer!*).

4.2.1   Harm and incompetence

The "not worse, and hopefully much better, off" standard directly reinforces the essential professional criterion of "skilled expert." Simply put, very few of the harms that emerge in professional contexts are *intentionally* caused; rather, they occur because of incompetence or negligence.

In many fields, incompetent service simply means inconvenience or added cost. In the professions – again, given what is at stake – incompetence can mean physical injury, economic devastation, ignorance, even death. You certainly want, for example, the person putting a sharp object into your brain to be highly skilled and knowledgeable!

The level of potential harm is also clearly connected to the nature of the professional activity. I routinely joke with my ethics students that they will probably get by just fine in life if I give them a wacky interpretation of Plato's allegory of the cave. But then I follow it up by reinforcing how critical it is that *they*, budding professionals all and especially those in the technical fields, be precise and accurate. The future structural engineers may be designing the bridge we shall all drive over, the robotics engineers may usher in the singularity, the bio-engineers could wreak real environmental havoc, and the software engineers can shatter a whole enterprise.

That last harm is exemplified in the October 2013 roll-out of healthcare.gov, the website built to facilitate initial sign-ups in the Affordable Care Act (ACA, or "Obamacare"). President Obama was in the midst of an especially good week politically. Congressional Republicans were tucking their tails between their legs over their failed attempt to cause a government shutdown and early reports had it that the ACA's health-care exchanges were going to allow millions of uninsured people to acquire affordable health coverage. The president was, in short, on a roll … until word started coming out that the website was at best dysfunctional. People could not get onto it, they experienced excessive delays, or they would get to the very end of an excruciatingly long process only to have the program freeze. It eventually took a "trauma team" of the nation's best computing and management experts weeks to get the site working.[4] The ACA was controversial enough and these problems were the last thing its (and the president's) critics needed. The program's legacy is certainly mixed,[5] but the website's initial failure left a stain of incompetence that continues to fuel its detractors – *and all because of inept programming.*

Failures like the ACA website, combined with the universal presence of digital software and hardware,[6] are among the motivations for a more formal professionalization of a wider array of computing jobs. Commonplace problems like the "blue screen of death" simply should not be acceptable, proponents of formal professionalization argue, within these increasingly vital fields.

Such incompetence-caused harms are, of course, not restricted to the technical fields. Inept legal counsel can mean imprisonment or severe economic loss, and unskilled mental health care can damage people for life – or worse. The molestation and Satanic abuse frenzy that rocked whole communities in the 1980s, for example, was attributable, to a great extent, to therapists who unwittingly created false "memories" in children or who relied on unproven and later largely disgraced theories of "repressed" memories (Pezdek and Banks, 1996). The associated hysteria tore families apart, resulted in prison time for people later deemed innocent, and damaged the reputation of law enforcement and professional counseling for years (Gross, 2012).

My goal here is not to regale you with horror stories; you can find plenty more with a simple online search. Rather, I hope the examples reinforce the core normativity of professionalism. Taking on this role, with its potential for serious harm and great good, entails accepting the associated responsibility to *do it right*, to be the skilled expert on whom others in real need can rely.

4.3   Cases

4.3.1   Mandatory vaccinations?

The year 2015 turned into that of the vaccination debate, after a late 2014 measles outbreak traced to Disneyland revealed that a significant percentage of California's school-aged children had not been immunized for the potentially deadly disease. The resulting media storm generated heated debate and eventual new legislation.

Parents opposed to mandatory vaccination cited questionable links to secondary illnesses, parental autonomy, and, less frequently, religious objections. Proponents noted the duty to beneficently protect other children, especially those with other medical conditions that preclude immunization and that make them all the more vulnerable to serious complications from measles. Prioritizing beneficence over parental autonomy, proponents also argued that the children of even the "anti-vax" parents need to have their welfare protected.

The California legislature responded in 2015 by passing a bill that removed existing language that allowed exemptions based on personal or religious beliefs. Health concerns, as identified by a licensed physician, are now the only qualifying exemption. Governor Jerry Brown signed the legislation, stating, "The science is clear that vaccines dramatically protect children against a number of infectious and dangerous diseases."

Opponents have continued to work to overturn the legislation, which took effect on July 1, 2016. Initial efforts to place an initiative on the ballot that would return the language to its original, broader verbiage failed, but other attempts continue. If you had the opportunity to vote for or against such a law, how would you vote and why?

4.3.2   How much should you give?

Assume that you live a comfortable life. You have a decent job; a roof over your head; indoor plumbing, heating, and cooling; and access to health care and educational opportunities. You also own a mobile phone with a voice and data plan, along with cable or streaming entertainment options. You also eat well; you certainly are not food insecure.

At the same time, you also know that there are millions of people around the world – even within your city – who do not live such a life. They do not know where their next meal is coming from or even if there will be a next meal. They cannot access health care or education and are thrilled just to luck out and get a few nights a week in a homeless shelter.

You also know that there are many aid organizations, both local and international, that do extraordinary work, with very low administrative overheads, to help such people. Do you have a duty of beneficence to donate some of your resources to these organizations? If so, what percentage of your resources would you give and why? What types of moral and prudential considerations should motivate your reasoning?

NOTES

1. Often mistaken as part of the Hippocratic Oath, it became dominant in medical ethics treatises in the mid- to late nineteenth century.
2. Singer's purpose with the scenario is to convince persons that they have a strict duty to help the "drowning child" elsewhere in the world, mainly by donating money to organizations whose various forms of life-saving assistance are highly effective.
3. James Rachels (1975) uses a similarly famous example to challenge many persons' gut feeling that active euthanasia is morally worse than passive. Assume that you intend to murder your nephew for his inheritance. You enter the bathroom as he is bathing with every intent to forcibly drown him (non-maleficence) but, upon your arrival, you see him slip and bump his head, falling face first into the water. You just stand there, gleefully taking in his predicament, when saving him would mean merely reaching down and lifting his head (beneficence). Most people's intuitions are that there is no morally significant difference between these acts.
4. Steven Brill's "Code Red" cover story for *Time Magazine* (Brill, 2014) does a masterful job of reporting why the website failed and what it took to get it working properly.
5. As of December 2016 some 20 million previously uninsured people, including those with pre-existing conditions, are now covered (US Department of Health and Human Services, 2016) and best estimates are that it has slowed down the rising cost of insurance premiums (Zamosky, 2016), but that 20 million is approximately half of original estimates and inflation in medical care is still far higher than the national average, with expenditures now up over $3 trillion a year (Alonso-Zaldivar, 2016).
6. Just try to go for two days having no digital involvement; you will almost certainly fail (your car is likely computerized, as is your phone, your GPS, your banking, your grocery store – you get the point).

REFERENCES

Ackerman, Terrence. 1982. "Why Doctors Should Intervene." *Hastings Center Report* 12 (4): 14–17.

Alonso, Zaldivar, Ricardo. 2016. "US Health Care Tab Hits $3.2T; Fastest Growth in 8 Years." Associated Press. http://www.msn.com/en-us/news/finance-insurance/us-health-care-tab-hits-dollar32t-fastest-growth-in-8-years/ar-AAl4c0S?ocid=se, accessed August 23, 2017.

Beauchamp, Tom, and Childress, James. 1977. *Principles of Biomedical Ethics.* New York: Oxford University Press.

Brill, Steven. 2014. "Obama's Trauma Team." *Time*, February 27, cover story.

Brooks, David. 2015. *The Road to Character.* New York: Random House.

Gross, Alexandra. 2012. "Brenda Kniffen: Other California Child Sex Abuse Hysteria Cases." National Registry of Exonerations. http://www.law.umich.edu/special/exoneration/pages/casedetail.aspx?caseid=3359, accessed August 23, 2017.

Lupton, Robert D. 2011. *Toxic Charity: How Churches and Charities Hurt Those They Help (And How to Reverse It).* San Francisco: HarperOne.

Pezdek, Kathy, and Banks, William P. 1996. *The Recovered Memory/False Memory Debate.* Waltham, MA: Academic Press.

Rachels, James. 1975. "Active and Passive Euthanasia." *New England Journal of Medicine* 292 (2): 78–80.

Schneider, Carl E. 1998. *The Practice of Autonomy: Patients, Doctors, and Medical Decisions.* New York: Oxford University Press.

Singer, Peter. 1997. "The Drowning Child and the Expanding Circle." *New Internationalist.* https://newint.org/features/1997/04/05/drowning, accessed August 23, 2017.

Singer, Peter. 2006. "Questions for Peter Singer." *New York Times Magazine.* http://www.nytimes.com/2006/12/24/magazine/24singerqa.html?mcubz=1, accessed September 1, 2017.

Singer, Peter. 2010. *The Life You Can Save: How to Do Your Part to End World Poverty.* New York: Random House.

US Department of Health and Human Services. 1979. "The Belmont Report." http://www.hhs.gov/ohrp/humansubjects/guidance/belmont.html, accessed August 23, 2017.

US Department of Health and Human Services. 2016. "20 Million People Have Gained Health Insurance Coverage because of the Affordable

Care Act, New Estimates Show." http://wayback.archive-it.org/3926/
20170127190440/https://www.hhs.gov/about/news/2016/03/03/20-
million-people-have-gained-health-insurance-coverage-because-
affordable-care-act-new-estimates, accessed August 23, 2017.

Veatch, Robert. 1981. *A Theory of Medical Ethics*. New York: Basic Books.

Zacharias, Fred C. 2001. "Limits on Client Autonomy in Legal Ethics Regulation." *Boston University Law Review* 81: 199, 211.

Zamosky, Lisa. 2016. "Health Premiums after Obamacare? They're Lower."
https://www.healthinsurance.org/blog/2016/07/29/health-premiums-
after-obamacare-theyre-lower, accessed August 23, 2017.

5 Competency

5.1 Systematizing Confidence   106

5.2 Case: Sanctioning a Colleague   111

     Note   112

An aspiring magician as well as a top-notch
surgeon, Dr. Curmbott always tried the old
tablecloth trick after each operation.

The Professional Ethics Toolkit, First Edition. Christopher Meyers.
© 2018 John Wiley & Sons Ltd. Published 2018 by John Wiley & Sons Ltd.

Recall our discussion from Chapter 1 about the distinction between instrumental and fiduciary relationships. In an instrumental relationship, you *may* get someone who is skilled and at least significantly concerned about your well-being; in a fiduciary relationship, your default is trust – you trust him because he has expressly committed himself to the moral norm of prioritizing your well-being *and* because you have the structural assurances that he is competent.

Your trust is assuredly enhanced – in either case – if the service provider has been recommended by friends or family. But what if you have no such recommendations and your needs are vital. For example, what if you are out of town and have a serious medical emergency, for which you need immediate medical care. Whatever trepidations you might have, the odds are that you would not refuse to be taken to the local emergency room just because you do not know anyone who has been treated there. Add the fact that you are in a major city and the hospital to which you are being taken is a high-level tertiary care hospital, and you would likely feel *very* confident, maybe even more than at your neighborhood primary care facility.

5.1   Systematizing Confidence

Such confidence is well and hard earned. The system that underlies professional training is demanding and far reaching. The universities that trained the hospital's health-care professionals devoted years and massive resources to getting it right. You know this because you also know that those training programs routinely undergo accreditation evaluations – both university wide and program specific. And the individual professionals have also undertaken lengthy, expensive, and intense training, culminating in the successful completion of their licensing exams, followed by ongoing, professionally mandated continuing education. Their respective professions are also self-regulating, with internal and external oversight of professional practice, including disciplinary action where needed.[1]

Furthermore, the hospital you are being rushed to is itself accredited, at least by the Joint Commission (formerly the Joint Commission on Accreditation of Healthcare Organizations [JCAHO]), and likely also by Centers for Medicare and Medicaid Services (CMS). Happily for patients, the reviews do not just assess the skill level of the practitioners but also whether the hospital follows the highest possible hygiene practices. They also look to make sure that the hospital has all the correct policies in place and that there is a correlation between those policies and what happens in the various wards. The standards by which the hospital is evaluated are dictated both nationally and regionally to ensure that it meets at least minimal national criteria and also the regional standard of care. Individual services within the hospital may also have separate accreditation and almost certainly do if they are also a teaching center, so that their medical residents or nursing trainees can, upon graduation, secure employment.

In short, if you want to see hospital administrators drop everything and focus all their attention on a small group of people, be present when the Joint Commission makes one of its (typically surprise) visits. And all this is very costly. In order to satisfy the noted standards, hospitals have to spend the money to ensure that they have, for example, all the required equipment (relative to their level of care), proper nursing-to-patient ratios, trained specialists available twenty-four hours a day and seven days a week, and the best hygiene protocols. This necessarily contributes to higher medical costs, as the hospital has to charge sufficiently high rates to be able to manage these ancillary expenses.

Now, it is likely that many of you had no idea that the health-care system is in fact this extensively regulated, internally and externally. You just take it for granted that, while there is of course some threat of error, the odds of that are relatively low and are certainly outweighed by the beneficent care you will almost certainly receive.

Health care is not alone in these requirements. Nearly all institutions of higher education also participate in their own version of accreditation, for example by the Western Association of Schools and Colleges and by the various professional groups that accredit the training programs for lawyers, engineers, architects, veterinarians, and so on, whom you will encounter in your lifetime.

Not surprisingly, there is considerable debate over whether these accreditation processes in fact result in higher-quality service. While universities' equipment and hygiene requirements are not as stringent as those for health-care facilities, their version of accreditation is still extraordinarily resource intensive, using up money and time that could be spent on other, more directly academic, needs, without a clear indication that educational and research services are correspondingly improved.

So why dedicate those resources to accreditation? Because doing so affirms the self-regulation requirement for all professions; such programs and institutions are showing with dollars how importantly they take that requirement. Fortunately, that investment also typically shows a good return. Clients of all stripes rightly have greater confidence in, and are more comfortable expending their resources on, accredited programs.

Again, it is very likely that you are not thinking about any of this as they wheel you into the treatment room – which is the goal. You should not *have* to worry about whether the person about to stitch you up – let alone rule out a heart attack or treat a hemorrhagic stroke – knows what they are doing. The system ensures that you can count on such professional expertise, or at least that incompetent behavior is the rare exception.

Contrast this confidence, though, with how you might feel in a rural section of a developing country. The professionals on duty may have at least as high a commitment to your well-being but not the resources – trained specialists and equipment – to give you the same level of care.

In sum, much of the trust we place in professionals is rooted in the individual and systemic commitment to fulfilling the central criteria of professionalism: to produce genuinely skilled experts who will look out for your well-being. In technical professions like engineering, the technical standards are relatively easier to establish and affirm: does the person know the math and the formulas necessary to get the design and development right? Similarly, one can determine in a pretty straightforward fashion whether one knows the relevant law in one's legal specialization; the same goes for the chemistry and other relevant literature in medicine. *How* one applies that knowledge, however, is harder to confirm; as noted, quality professional service is as much art as techne.

Further, even the knowledge-based and technical standards in other professions are more amorphous. What are the objective criteria, for example, for whether a professor inspires her students, or even whether her out-of-the-ordinary interpretation of a classic text is within bounds and thus protected by academic freedom? Maybe it is just an absurd reading that should never be taught to students? How does one objectively evaluate whether she is a good campus and community citizen, or has sufficiently original and well-written ideas to be considered a true scholar? Many academic disciplines have tried to rely on objective standards – for example, a certain percentage of favorable student reviews, a minimum number of publications in journals with acceptable ranking metrics, and a defined number of committee memberships. So much of what academics do well, though, is not quantifiable in these ways. The creativity and commitment necessary to be a skilled professor just do not easily reduce to the quantitative, making qualitative assessments more appropriate. Such qualitative judgments are also ill suited to assuring potential clients, let alone accrediting bodies, of one's skilled expertise – hence the (over-)reliance on quantitative data.

The academy is not alone in its struggles with providing objective evidence that confirms client trust. Beyond basic structural and safety requirements, how does one evaluate the creative achievements of an architect? Is Frank Gehry's vision brilliantly creative or just plain weird? Does the successful litigator win so often because he knows the law better than his opponents or because he knows how to communicate in a way that resonates with jurors? The best palliative care physicians certainly know their chemistry and which drugs are likely to be most effective for specific conditions, but they also – probably even more – know how to *talk* and to *listen*, as their patients move into the dying process. Even the best programmers, whose work is completely dependent on straightforward and objective logic, are also very creative in their coding – creative in a way that is near impossible to quantify or to teach others.

Add to these the professions where there is no consensus on theory and thus where evidence of competency is all the harder to determine. As noted, university-level teaching is high on that list; most of us who have been doing it for many years never took a class in teaching theory or method or even read the associated literature. Pick up a book on mental health ethics and you will notice the attention given to the relationship between questionable therapeutic theory and the significant harm that clients may suffer. Other professions, of course, discuss the harm the professional can cause in the course of his work, but theoretical underpinnings are more firmly established, with practice standards following suit.

Does this mean that there is no mechanism for assessing competency in the more subjective, more artful, professions? Of course not. There are clear minimum standards that every practicing professional must meet – those established for entry to the field. Beyond that, reputational appraisals are vital. Assuming that you had a choice, you would very likely not seek mental health counseling without a recommendation from a trusted friend or colleague. Likewise if you have options as to which particular professor's class to take or which architect to hire.

Nothing can damage a profession more than widespread incompetence. Clients must be able to assume without question that the person from whom they are seeking help on a vital matter is in fact truly a skilled expert. Professions have the privilege and the responsibility of self-regulation, of guaranteeing that one cannot practice – for most, this means licensing – without having met at least the minimum standards. Further, continuing education requirements and ongoing peer review are meant to ensure that practitioners stay up to date with the latest knowledge and techniques, and sanctions may be imposed where necessary.

Do these mechanisms work? Yes and no. The standards for admission as a practicing member of all the professions listed in Chapter 1 are rigorous and well managed, not least because very lucrative businesses have developed around associated programs.

It is *tough* to become a doctor, a lawyer, a licensed therapist, a professional engineer, and even a university-level philosopher. One must undertake many years of education and extensive disciplinary training, and pass a barrage of exams before being certified to practice on one's own.

Once in that position, however, the self-regulatory procedures are more questionable. Consider, for example, how skeptical most university students are about whether their course evaluations make a difference for a tenured full professor; their sense is that such faculty staff are beyond challenge. And, realistically, they are not far off. Such faculty can be positively *induced* to do better but negative sanctions, in other than truly egregious cases, are rare. Peer review committees in medicine and law have greater authority but are not widely used – there are just too many cultural, practical, and power-related constraints that militate against reporting one's colleagues.

As noted, we shall explore in the Epilogue how these concerns contributed to the democratization movement of the 1970s and also consider how self-regulation could be more reliable.

5.2   Case: Sanctioning a Colleague

Imagine that you are a recently hired assistant professor at a university that prioritizes teaching above research. It is a small department and everyone has to teach a range of areas, including ones in which they were not originally trained. You are anxious about, but also excited by, the prospect of becoming sufficiently knowledgeable in some new areas that you will teach in the spring semester. You decide to sit in on a couple of class sessions taught by one of your colleagues, April, to learn more about some historical figures you will be discussing in those classes. April has a reputation for highly unorthodox beliefs about the paranormal and the afterlife, but you are not concerned because they are well outside the topics she will be covering. You note that your other colleagues do not particularly respect her, but laugh her off as "quirky." They, and she, are all founding faculty members of the department, so there is also a kind of familial culture at work, with widespread affection for all the members – even for April.

You sit in on the first class session and are quickly alarmed. Not only does she know even less about the philosophers she is teaching than you do, but she has consistently found a way to bring in comments about the paranormal, even though they have no coherent connection to the topics at hand. You suspect that she was doing that in part to try to impress you, to win you over as an ally, and this makes you all the angrier. The students were at best being short-changed, at worst receiving an incompetent lecture.

You find your most trusted colleague later that day and seek his advice. To your disappointment, he says, "Oh, that's just April. Don't let her get to you." He then convinces you to attend the second session, as planned: "Maybe she was just off her game today. And, besides, you really don't want to get on her bad side – she will of course be on your tenure review committee."

You do, in fact, attend the second class and are even more disturbed. The content was no better, the paranormal references no less frequent, and this time she made a few comments you found subtly demeaning to women and non-whites. You did not see any visible reaction from students when she voiced those comments, but you had to think that at least some of them picked up on them.

You go back to your friend and this time he is considerably more serious: "Look, you would be hard-pressed to make any of this stick and even if you did, she's a tenured full professor – what can anyone do? The rest of us have learned to live with her; you can too. And, just to make sure you heard it the first time, she will be on your review committee. And you know that she regularly golfs with the provost, right? Let it go."

What should you do?

NOTE

1. As I shall discuss in the Epilogue, part of the democratizing push back against the professions has been driven by a (justified) lack of confidence in that self-regulating function.

6

Confidentiality and Privacy

6.1	Privacy	115
6.2	Privacy as a Moral Root of Confidentiality	116
6.3	Practical Considerations	120
6.4	Cases	122
	Notes	124
	References	125

Think for a moment about your closest friend, the person with whom you share your most intimate secrets. Imagine you tell him – only after making him promise to keep it confidential – that you had a brief, alcohol-fueled romantic encounter with a stranger you picked up at a bar. You are pretty ashamed about it and are just hoping to forget the whole thing. You are counting on your friend to give you

The Professional Ethics Toolkit, First Edition. Christopher Meyers.
© 2018 John Wiley & Sons Ltd. Published 2018 by John Wiley & Sons Ltd.

a good – "What were you thinking?" – talking to. He does, but, much to your horror, he also later posts the story on Facebook, complete with an old photo of you taken at a party when you were totally blitzed. Assuming, that no one was hurt and there was no infidelity involved, no lasting harm beyond deep embarrassment would likely result. You would probably just dump your friend and warn others to keep their distance (while maybe also getting some substance abuse counseling).

Now imagine that the confidant is your attorney and you are discussing something that could put you in real legal jeopardy. Not only does she post it in on Facebook but, just to make sure, she also gives all the details to opposing counsel. Here the revelation could mean real economic loss, even jail time. It also would almost certainly mean the attorney would be legally sanctioned, probably even disbarred.

In both cases your privacy has been invaded but, consistent with the professional designation, the second impacted a *vital matter*, one that could have a profound bearing on your life and well-being. It is precisely for this reason that the principle of confidentiality is so basic to the professional–client relationship. Trust, the foundation of these relationships, can exist only where there is an explicit and demanding expectation of confidentiality.

Rooted most directly in the moral concept of privacy but also in pragmatic and utilitarian considerations of what makes for effective professional–client communication, confidentiality is a core role-based ethical principle in every profession. It also carries stringent professional sanction when violated, in part because such violations can occur only intentionally or via negligence.

In this chapter we shall discuss what privacy/confidentiality is, that is, how it is best understood conceptually. We shall also explore why privacy (and thus confidentiality) is such a vital moral concern, especially in professional settings, with particular emphasis on its connection to autonomy and to social utility. While it is vital, however, confidentiality does not carry absolute value – even in such settings as criminal law or mental health, where it is often taken to be inviolable.

---------------------------------- 6.1   Privacy ----------------------------------

Outside of professional and personal settings, privacy seems to be quickly becoming little more than a quaint idea. Consider, for example, the ubiquitous collection of electronic data, including on-line searches, purchases, and conversations. And just try to opt out of such data collection (e.g., by refusing cookies). Not only is it often very difficult to achieve, but the companies' and agencies' response, as often as not, is the equivalent of "Fine – if you don't want us to collect your data, don't use our services." Furthermore, as social media usage suggests, contemporary youths place a lower value on privacy, maybe in part because they have become resigned to its inevitable invasion. Even in professional settings, where privacy is highly valued, there are any number of circumstances in which revelation is not only allowed but is legally and ethically mandated.

This chapter will explore some of those instances and discuss how to evaluate other situations that are similar but not as clear cut. We shall also address the practical side of confidentiality – namely, how mundane activities, for example elevator talk, are among the most pernicious threats. We will close with cases that exemplify the principle's importance and also how difficult it can be to balance confidentiality against other key values.

Before addressing the conceptual and definitional analyses, this is an important place to reinforce the differences between legal and ethical approaches. As discussed in Chapter 2, legal considerations contribute in important ways to understanding the *facts* of the matter, but they do not end the ethics conversation. Instead, they generally represent a minimal and pragmatically achievable standard. Privacy is a paradigm example of that broad sweeping attempt to balance associated ethical concerns.

Legal approaches focus on two concerns: *where* was the information revealed and *who* was the information about? The where question gets at whether one can have a reasonable expectation that others will not have access to the information. This gets played out in interesting, and sometimes troubling ways. For example, in its attempt to meet a range of values and needs, particularly with respect to news and entertainment media, the law establishes a basic minimum standard for what counts as "public": if an event occurs in a public setting or can be seen or heard without technological enhancement (e.g., telescopic lens and parabolic microphones), then the participants have no associated legal right to privacy. This holds regardless of whether the participants *chose* to engage in that activity or wished to have their, sometimes very intimate, activities publicly broadcast, displayed, or reported. Consider the ever-present news stories of accident or crime victims, people who may desperately want their information kept private but who do not have that legal option because the event occurred in a public setting.

The who question gets at the role of the person about whom information is being revealed: are they a so-called public figure, someone who has intentionally chosen to place themselves in the spotlight (politicians and celebrities are the most common)? If so, the law generally declares that they have little to no protection against information revelations, since they voluntarily put themselves out there and since they often directly benefit from public awareness (Gauthier, 2010).

This kind of meat cleaver approach may be the best the law can do, given the range of competing interests, but for individuals, especially individual professionals, a finer scalpel is needed, relying on the sorts of distinctions provided in section 6.2.

—— 6.2 Privacy as a Moral Root of Confidentiality ——

Think back to the case at the beginning of this chapter and the sense of betrayal you would have felt at your friend's revelation. In simple terms, the depth of your hurt can be traced to the fact that he *is* your closest friend. Take a different version of the story. You are back at the same bar a week later, chatting with a mere acquaintance. You notice last week's temporary companion across the room and point him out to this acquaintance, deriding yourself for your poor choice.

Should *this* conversation turn up on Facebook, you would kick yourself for being stupid enough to share such intimacies with a relative stranger, but you would probably not, or at least you should not, feel *betrayed* (assuming that you did not ask for or receive a promise of confidentiality).

Betrayal is directly connected to trust, an attitude over which, in most personal relationships, we have near-complete control. It is also central to and reflective of the kind of relationship we have with someone. In personal relationships we *decide* whether to trust someone, whether to reveal our private intimacies to them. Those decisions are, in fact, key to how we define our loves and friendships. Charles Fried nicely captures this point in a prescient discussion about governmental monitoring of citizens:

> [Privacy] forms the necessary context for the intimate relations of love and friendship ... In the role of citizen or fellow worker, one need reveal himself to no greater extent than is necessary to display the attributes of competence and morality appropriate to those roles. In order to be a friend or lover, one must reveal far more of himself. Yet where any intimate revelation may be heard by monitoring officials, it loses the quality of *exclusive intimacy* required of a gesture of love or friendship. Thus [governmental] monitoring, in depriving one of privacy, destroys the possibility of *bestowing the gift* of intimacy, and makes impossible the essential dimension of love and friendship. (Fried, 1970, 147–148; emphases added)

6.2.1 Intimacy and confidentiality

To share an intimacy with someone is to give a gift, one that creates real *exposure* by opening up the most vulnerable parts of our personality, character, and history – the intimacies that serve as the foundation of love and friendship. But notice in Fried's quotation the implied *control* over information: persons *choose* with whom to share intimate facts, in part because through doing so we thereby define our relationships. Generally speaking, the more detail provided (and expected), the closer the relationship.[1]

This can be seen when considering the converse of our opening story. Imagine that your closest friend has recently gone through a traumatic experience but you learn of it from someone your friend barely knows. Wouldn't you likely react with: "What the heck? You told him but not me? I thought we were friends!" Or, often, even more troublingly, you ask one of those mere acquaintances, in typical rote fashion, "How's it going?" *and they tell you*: they start recounting, say, an intimate medical procedure or that their partner had an affair last weekend. Your reaction, very likely, will be something along the lines of, "Oh, ick. Dude, we're not that close."

6.2.2   Deontological and utilitarian foundations

But why should we care whether others have access to our private information? Especially when it is easy enough to see that people vary considerably on the relative importance they give to privacy, as well as on what information they want protected. While almost everyone would prefer, for instance, that their bathroom activities be kept private, there is considerable variation on such matters as public displays of affection, media coverage of tragedy, and even financial information.[2]

The value of privacy is grounded in a number of important deontological and utilitarian principles (Gauthier, 2010). First, revelation of, for example, financial information can result in a violation of one's deontological *right to property*, while also creating utility-damaging distrust in a banking system that is necessary to social commerce. Second, our ability to form and sustain *autonomous life plans* is in important ways directly connected with our ability to form and sustain intimate relationships. Such relationships provide the emotional and often physical and financial support that undergirds life's choices. Third, as we have been discussing throughout this book, professional–client relationships are grounded in *trust*, including trust that private information is sacrosanct.

That trust is all the more critical given the *forced* intimacy of professional–client relationships. In order to achieve the outcomes for which you are seeking professional help, you often have to reveal deeply private information, sometimes information that you would not share with your closest friend. The associated vulnerability is, furthermore, just as profound, maybe even more so, since you do not really have a choice about the revelation – doing so is critical to your interaction. And, since there is less choice involved, you simply *must* be able to trust that the professional will keep the information confidential.

If you do not have that trust, you might not seek professional help in the first place, with correspondingly negative impacts on your well-being and on aggregate social utility (we all certainly want our contagious neighbors and co-workers to seek medical assistance). Or, even if you did seek help but did not have enough trust to reveal everything, the professional would be less able to work effectively with you.

Defense attorneys, for example, describe their frustration when clients withhold information out of fear that it will hurt their case. As these attorneys note, clients are often mistaken about what helps or hurts and the worst outcome is being surprised by the prosecution's presentation of previously unknown evidence. "Just tell me everything," they say, "and I'll figure out how or whether to use it."[3] Similarly, imagine going to your physician because you are not feeling well and not telling her about your recent chest pains, or talking to your collegiate adviser about changing your major to physics but not telling him that you have a math phobia.

To sum up: Confidentiality is critical to professional–client relationships for both deontological (its contribution to the ability to form and fulfill an autonomous life plan) and utilitarian reasons (without it, persons would be less likely to seek help from professionals, with corresponding social harms). It is also a tough principle for professionals to follow, given the noted variability on what sorts of information different people consider private. Part of the challenge, thus, is to determine how individual clients feel about the revelation of specific information; barring that, the safe fallback position is to protect information as far as possible, unless told otherwise.

Confidentiality is also among the most frequently stressed professional ethics principles in education and in practice. Consider, for example, the US (Federal) Health Insurance Portability and Accountability Act of 1996 (HIPAA), with the strenuous privacy demands it places upon health-care professionals and organizations.

Given its dominant presence in professional ethics, why, then, is confidentiality so frequently violated? And it is – in elevators, in lunch-time conversations, and in snarky comments professionals share with one another.

6.3   Practical Considerations

Not surprisingly, there are good and not so good reasons for these violations. Professionals are, like everyone else, curious people, anxious to add stimulating conversations to their daily lives. So they talk and, naturally, they talk about their work and the people involved. Some of that talk is necessary – consultative and educational; some is closer to gossip. And they talk in a variety of places and environments – sometimes with due care that they cannot be overheard; sometimes in hallways or corridors, unaware that the stranger next to them happens to know the person they are discussing. They also put confidential information in writing – sometimes very carefully, with signature lines describing legal privacy requirements; sometimes sloppily, for example listing patients on a semi-public white board, with disease details and personal information.

Even in legitimate educational and consultative contexts – for example, bringing in an expert to discuss the client's circumstances – there are better and worse ways to protect confidentiality. This was brought home to me many years ago. The patient in a case on which I was providing ethics consultation turned out to be a friendly acquaintance. He had contracted a serious illness that was having a devastating impact on his brain, reducing his cognitive capacities to those of a young child. It was unclear at that point whether he would recover and I was very confident that he would not want his circumstances to be widely known, including by peripheral members of his social circle – like me. This motivated me to reinforce with the physicians that we use patient numbers only when discussing cases; even initials can be revealing when provided along with personal details.

Other common violations include using cases to illustrate key concepts or principles educationally without sufficiently disguising them. Even in a book like this, it would be easy enough to unintentionally violate someone's confidentiality. One never knows who one's readers will be. Thus, while, as noted at the outset, many of the examples and cases described herein are based on actual ones I have encountered, I have worked hard to anonymize them.

6.3.1   Weighing confidentiality against other principles

As the foregoing discussion suggests, most violations of confidentiality occur negligently, as a result of sloppiness rather than malevolence. Ill-intentioned purposeful violations also occur, of course, but they are by far the exception. The primary professional ethics lesson, thus, is diligent attention: be aware of what you say (or write), where, and to whom.

Can there ever be justified intentional violations? Of course. As we saw in Chapter 2, the hard work of ethics reasoning involves figuring out the proper balance when principles conflict. Tempting as it is to treat any of the mid-level or practice principles as absolute – tempting because it saves one from having to do that hard reasoning work – no principle has that kind of moral force.

Some justified confidentiality violations are easy, even legally mandated. Evidence of child abuse, gunshot wounds, a diagnosis of a sexually transmitted disease, communications that are clearly terrorism engendering, and "Tarasoff" cases (in which a client reveals confidential information that the professional should reasonably interpret as a threat to another person)[4] – any of these represents a (justified) privacy/confidentiality violation if one assumes, as outlined in our earlier discussion, that the relevant person would not choose to have that information revealed; left to her, it would be kept confidential.

I have had professionals try to claim that these do not, in fact, represent a breach of confidentiality, since, they argue, the client has no *right* to the information being protected, given the actual or potential harm associated with its protection. Notice, though, that this position is a *conclusion*, one based on a reasoned analysis that other ethical considerations outweigh, in these cases the person's privacy: protection of children, law enforcement concerns, disease prevention, and public safety (or, translated into principles language, non-maleficence, formal justice, beneficence, and aggregate social utility, respectively). To say that something is a breach of confidentiality is a factual and conceptual claim; whether it is a *warranted* breach is an ethical claim, one that can be reached only via sufficient reasoned analysis.

Let me thus provide a couple of cases for you to do exactly that.

6.4   Cases

6.4.1   Balancing principles: Privacy, beneficence, non-maleficence, honesty, and fidelity

You are a licensed clinical social worker and have been doing family counseling sessions with the Joneses – Bill and Susie and their fifteen-year-old daughter, Jennifer – for about six months. You have an explicit understanding that confidentiality extends only externally; conversations within the family will be shared with all family members.

It is not unusual for you to meet separately with each of the family members as you have found that you often get a more nuanced and deeper insight into problems when you can talk to them individually. Today you have Jennifer alone and, before you can get to some issues raised in last week's family session, she says, "I have to talk with you about something important: I am two months pregnant. I got drunk at a party and had sex with two guys. I've already scheduled the appointment for an abortion, but wanted to talk with you first – you seem to know so much about so many issues."

You are pretty flabbergasted. Jennifer has always come across as a pretty innocent and naive girl and that is certainly the impression her parents have of her – to their great joy and satisfaction. Both are quite conservative, with evangelical Christian beliefs. Bill has, on multiple occasions, made disparaging and bigoted comments about "those slutty girls just trying to milk the welfare system by having a kid."

Before you can delve deeper into Jennifer's issues, including your desire to find out more about the two boys (given that they may in fact have committed assault), she says: "You of course can't tell *anyone*. If my dad found out, he'd kill me!" While you think this may be an exaggeration, you also recognize that Bill has a serious temper. They are, in fact, in court-ordered family therapy because Bill slapped Susie in front of Jennifer. And Susie is no shrinking violet: she has thrown dishes at Bill on more than one occasion.

You are in a real bind. You have a family session scheduled for three days from now, and during those sessions the first topic of conversation has always been whatever came up in the individual meetings. While you have made real progress of late, you realize that this revelation could take you back to square one – even do real harm to the family relationships, making things worse than when they first came to you.

Which duty should prevail here? Your beneficent commitment to help Jennifer resolve this tough issue and to protect her from potential harm from her family? Your duty of confidentiality to each member of the family? Your duty of honesty and fidelity to maintain the promise of full truth? Your beneficent duty to protect other potential victims of the boys and your associated duty of justice to see that they are properly punished (should that be appropriate)? Or something else?

6.4.2 Tell the family?

Among the most famous legal cases in US history involved two upstate New York attorneys, Frank Armani and Francis Belge, and their decision to zealously protect their client's confidentiality.[5]

In 1973 Armani and Belge were appointed by the court to represent Robert Garrow for the murder of Philip Domblewski, an eighteen-year-old college student. In their initial interviews, Garrow did exactly what defense attorneys want. He told them everything that was relevant to the case, including that he had killed Domblewski. Furthermore, he told them, he had in a separate incident killed another camper, along with his girlfriend, whom he had also abducted and raped. He went on to tell them of the abduction, rape, and murder of yet another teenaged girl. Garrow even told his lawyers where he had dumped the bodies of his two female victims, which they confirmed by going to the sites and taking pictures of the remains.

During the trial, Garrow eventually confessed to killing Domblewski, as well as to the other murders and rapes, along with a number of rapes and abductions throughout upstate New York. The day after Garrow finished testifying, Armani and Belge acknowledged publicly that they had known all along about the murders and the locations of the victims' bodies, but their duty of confidentiality prevented them from revealing the information, even when the parents of one of the girls directly requested it.

The remainder of the story is complex and troubling (Hansen, 2007), but the question for our purposes is straightforward: did the lawyers act ethically in protecting Garrow's confidentiality?

NOTES

1. "Generally" because there is also the "seat mate" phenomenon, in which persons share sometimes quite personal information with complete strangers – the person sitting next to them on an airplane, for example. The likely explanation for this is that it is almost an anonymous disclosure – these two people will likely never cross paths again and thus there is, in fact, little or no vulnerability attached to disclosure.

2. I give my students an exercise in which they indicate how concerned they would be by the revelation of a range of information, including such things as "images of the mess in your car," "your bank account number," "details of your most recent sexual experience," "details about conflicts with your family," and "images of you nude as a baby." While over the

years there has been considerable overlap, there are always strong minorities on both ends of the spectrum.

3. For those unfamiliar with criminal proceedings, the prosecution is generally required to reveal all the evidence they have gathered, while the defense may generally keep it confidential.
4. *Tarasoff v. Regents of University of California*, 17 Cal.3d 425, 131 Cal.Rptr. 14, 551 P.2d 334 (1976).
5. What follows is taken liberally from Hansen (2007).

REFERENCES

Fried, Charles. 1970. *An Anatomy of Values*. Cambridge, MA: Harvard University Press.

Gauthier, Candace. 2010. "Understanding and Respecting Privacy." In *Journalism Ethics: A Philosophical Approach*, edited by Christopher Meyers, 215–230. New York: Oxford University Press.

Hansen, Mark. 2007. "The Toughest Call." ABA Journal, August 1. http://www.abajournal.com/magazine/article/the_toughest_call, accessed August 24, 2017.

7

Conflict of Interest

7.1   Definition   128

7.2   Types of Conflicting Inducements   132

7.3   Structural Conflict of Interest   136

7.4   Cases   140

        Notes   143

        References   144

The Professional Ethics Toolkit, First Edition. Christopher Meyers.
© 2018 John Wiley & Sons Ltd. Published 2018 by John Wiley & Sons Ltd.

Imagine that you are the plaintiff in a complex civil case, one in which the stakes for you are quite high, including the potential loss of your family business. After nearly three weeks, the trial is winding down and, from your vantage point, it seems to be going pretty well. You had hoped for more from your lead attorney, but you are optimistic that, unless something goes awry in the final days, the jury will largely rule in your favor.

Your husband convinces you to take a break from the tension and have a quiet dinner at a nice, out-of-the-way restaurant. He was right – after a wonderful meal, you are feeling much more relaxed as you sip an after-dinner brandy. You happen, though, to look across the room and who do you see at an almost hidden table way in the back? Your attorney, and he is with opposing counsel! Given the long gazes and physical affection each is showing the other, it is clear that they are romantically involved. You gulp your brandy, drop plenty of cash on the table, and grab your husband to head out before he can see you.

You stop by his office early the next morning to confront him about what you saw. To your great surprise, however, his reaction is not at all what you expected. He is almost giddy as he exclaims, "Yes, we just got together! Isn't she amazing? Look, whatever else comes of this trial, you can be happy that you helped two lonely people find love."

You look at him aghast and reply, "Good for you, but what about the conflict of interest?" He responds: "What conflict? As you know, I'm on contingency fee, so the better we do in the case, the more I make. And she's on retainer, so has no skin in the game." You are flabbergasted at his naivety but feel stuck. You consider firing him and switching to his associate, who has been second chair throughout the trial, but their obviously close, mentor–mentee relationship makes you doubt whether he could take over without repercussion. And you certainly do not want to have to get a new lawyer and start all over again, even assuming that the judge would allow that. You decide that you are stuck and just hope for the best.

The jury does find the defendants mostly liable, awarding you 65 percent of what you had requested – obviously well below what you had hoped and considerably below what you thought the evidence showed. In fact, on the way out, you hear the defendants say to each other, "Whew, dodged a bullet there."

Your attorney, standing next to you, hears it too. You glare at him and walk quickly away. He later sends you a note carefully outlining why this was, in fact, the best outcome you could have hoped for. He makes a compelling argument but you are left forever wondering whether the relationship had an impact on the outcome of the trial.

Are such doubts warranted? Almost assuredly, yes. This section will explain why they are by, first, defining conflict of interest; second, discussing why it is a, maybe *the*, central problem in professional ethics; third, analyzing what makes for structural conflicts of interest and how to manage them; and, fourth, exploring the concept in a few cases.

7.1 Definition

A conflict of interest emerges as the result of damaged trust within a fiduciary relationship, that is, within relationships where the affected party trusts the professional to act with her best interest in mind. Recall that the normative foundation of the professional–client relationship demands that the professional prioritize the client's well-being. When something – material gain, increased power or status, sexual inducement, or relational quid pro quo – interferes with this moral focus, a conflict of interest is present. To quote Michael Davis, a conflicting "interest is any influence, loyalty, concern, emotion, or other feature of a situation tending to make the professional's judgment (in that situation) less reliable than it would normally be" (2005, 2).[1]

Note that this definition allows one to give attention either to the *individual* (What is his moral, emotional, and psychological response to the interference and how does that impact his commitment to client well-being?) or to the *situation* (Are the circumstances such that one would assume that the parties' judgment will be altered?).

7.1.1 Situational conflict of interest

Both foci are, as we shall see, important, but many scholars concentrate on the latter, believing it to be a more objective standard. One need only look at the circumstantial conditions to know that there is at least a strong potential for conflict (Brody, 2005). Approaching conflicts from this direction – assessing the situation, not the individuals – saves one the difficult task of trying to get inside the agent's head to interpret her thoughts or feelings. Better, proponents argue, to encourage the creation of work environments that deter conflicting interferences – see, for example, the decision by academic medical centers to restrict the role of pharmaceutical representatives, especially their gift giving or program sponsorship (Brennan et al., 2006; Elliott, 2004).

Further support for the situational approach to conflicts of interest comes with the recognition that the circumstances in which such choices emerge bring their own norms: culture, history, and power structures all contribute to – maybe even dictate – how those who are involved perceive the facts of the matter (Mower, 2014). As Philip Zimbardo wrote:

> Good people can be induced, seduced, and initiated into behaving in evil ways ... We want to believe in the essential, unchanging goodness of people, in their power to resist external pressures ... The SPE ... reveals a message we do not want to accept: that most us can undergo significant character transformations when we are caught up in the crucible of social forces ... This lesson should have been taught repeatedly by the behavioral transformation of Nazi concentration camp guards, and of those in destructive cults. [These and similarly horrific group actions] also provide strong evidence of people surrendering their humanity and compassion to social power and abstract ideologies ... The primary simple lesson the Stanford Prison Experiment teaches is that *situations matter*. Social situations can have more profound effects on the behavior and mental functioning of individuals, groups, and national leaders than we might believe possible. Some situations

can exert such powerful influence over us that we can be led to behave in ways we would not, could not, predict was possible in advance. (2008, 211–212).

The impact of organizational cultures can be profound (Meyers, 2004; Werhane, 1999), truly altering how members of those cultures view ethical matters, including what counts as a conflicting interest. Creating more ethically sound work environments, hence, is clearly central to ethical practices and to avoiding conflicts of interest.

7.1.2   Conflict of interest and individual choices

At the same time, however, focusing on those cultures takes the risk of effectively painting all associated professionals with the same brush, essentially saying: "We don't know which of our members are have such high moral standards that their judgment cannot be negatively impacted, so we'll simply preclude all forms of inducements."

Many professionals are deeply offended when one even suggests that their judgment may be altered so easily. I once had a ballroom full of physicians who were enraged by the suggestion that they should not accept *any* gifts from drug representatives, given their potential to negatively impact their prescribing patterns. And, on the face of it, it does look like you are making that accusation; why else would you be concerned about any or all of them having their judgment altered?

The appropriate response to such perceived insult is to point out that you are not suggesting they are *corrupt* but rather that they are *human*. Humans, psychological research shows, have a wonderful tendency toward reciprocity. When someone receives a gift, they typically (if also often subconsciously) feel a strong inclination to give something in return (Mower, 2014). This natural trait is, in fact, one of humanity's great social lubricants, motivating appreciation and gratitude for the generosity of others and thereby enhancing communal bonds. At the same time, however, it can also – and again often subconsciously does – serve to alter a professional's normal judgment in a way that is potentially detrimental to her client.

That one may not even be aware of the altered judgment is another reason that many prefer to just focus on the situation, not on the professional's psychological state. If they are sometimes not even aware of the conflict of interest, how can outsiders be? We should, the argument goes, just attempt to create the right conditions, ones in which judgment-altering inducements are eliminated or at least reduced.

This situational approach is, again, vital, but it does not go far enough. As we shall discuss in more detail in section 7.3, some professional situations are unavoidably conflicting. There are *structural* conflicts of interest built into the very nature of some professional activities (e.g., when professionals are paid on an hourly basis, thereby creating an unavoidable inducement to extend the work).

7.1.3   Psychology and character

We thus return to the psychological and characterological component. Individual professionals must be especially *aware* of the various judgment-altering inducements that are present in their lives and to *resist* them as far as possible. Given how tempting these can often be – most people are only partially aware of the range of motives driving their choices, including those that are subtle inducements – the ethical professional also relies on the trusted colleagues to serve as a sounding board, even a reinforcing conscience. A variation on this, which can be employed when no such colleague is available, is the so-called 60-minute test: how comfortable would you be explaining your motives and reasoning if an aggressive reporter showed up at your office door to challenge you on a given decision, practice, or relationship?

In sum, and slightly amending our definition, a conflict of interest is present when the professional's judgment has been altered in a way that detracts from his acting or advising in his client's best interest, recognized either through discerning self-reflection, through the judgment of objective outsiders, or through awareness that situational circumstances create a high potential for altered judgment.

———— ## 7.2 Types of Conflicting Inducements ————

7.2.1 Material inducements

The most widely recognized inducement is material gain – money or other material goods. Actual cash bribes are unusual in professional–client relationships, but gifts of goods or services are fairly common. Many such gifts are just that – sincere expressions of appreciation or gratitude. And, if they come after that fact, after any professional judgment or action has been fulfilled, they are wholly appropriate.

Inappropriate inducements typically involve the offer of a good or service that could sway the decision in a direction other than that which is in the client's best interest or that harms other clients. Consider, for example, the failing student who offers his professor a nice bottle of scotch at the end of the term. This transparent attempt at acquiring an unfair advantage is both against his interest (the whole point of the course is to acquire the knowledge and skills, not just to get a particular grade) and can harm others (if the professor grades on a curve, meaning that any enhancement of his score will hurt others). In short, the proffered gift represents a direct attempt to alter the professional's judgment in a way that ultimately serves *no one's* interest.

Similarly, when drug representatives offer physicians a gift, they are of course also attempting to curry favor, to encourage a positive attitude and response. Yes, they are also assuredly providing vital information to overworked professionals who do not have the time to keep up with the literature. But it would be naive to think that the representative is not there, first and foremost, to promote her and her company's interest. "Her" is used consciously here, since drug reps are frequently very attractive women, chosen in part because the company knows that they will be more successful in gaining male physicians' attention.

Pharmaceutical companies are not driven by the professional norm of prioritizing their clients' well-being. They are providing a vital service – developing and disseminating needed, even life-saving, drugs. But they are, in the end, profit driven, as beholden to shareholders as much as, or even more than, physicians and patients. They are also quite good at such profit, consistently producing annual returns in the 15 to 20 percent range, industry wide. When they spend money on marketing and promotion ($12 *billion* in 2005), it is not as a community service. Rather, they know that those dollars are an investment, ultimately bringing in a far higher return in increased sales. They know this because they are quite familiar with the research that shows how even minor inducements – for example, logo pens and notepads – motivate changes in prescribing patterns that cannot be otherwise explained (Katz et al., 2003).

The upshot? Although it is very difficult to show a causal connection, there is a strikingly strong correlation between a drug representative's visit and gift and altered prescribing patterns – even when the change is detrimental to the client and when there is no additional plausible explanation for the change (Katz et al., 2003). Imagine, thus, what the old practice of giving high-prescribing physicians exotic trips and expensive meals accomplished!

7.2.2 Perceived conflict of interest

Many professionals, assuredly, are unaffected by such inducements, or at least so minimally affected that they do not produce detrimental choices for their clients. But *perception* also plays a key role here. If, in the first case, other students hear of the bribe attempt, even if it fails, they are likely to at least wonder about the professor's fairness ("Why would he think a bribe would work unless he had heard something?"). Similarly, if you know that a range of treatment options are available and you notice your physician writing a prescription for the most expensive drug using that company's logo pen, would you question the motivation behind that choice?

It is because of the actual and the perceived impact of gift giving that many groups have strict rules about the acceptance of gifts. For example, as a general rule, members of the US Executive Branch may not accept any gift worth more than $20, or $50 annually, from the same source (US Office of Government Ethics). The *New York Times* discourages *all* gifts or gratuities, except where it is not practical or feasible to reject them (New York Times, 2004). And, in the case of politicians, the mere appearance of a conflict of interest can deeply damage their constituents' trust, preventing them from being able to be an effective representative; that is, in such cases, the mere *appearance* of a conflict has the same negative impact as an *actual* conflict.[2]

7.2.3   Conflicts of obligation and bias

In addition to material conflicts of interest, professionals' judgment can also be altered by conflicts of obligation. Recall our discussion of role-based duties and imagine being in a role (or roles) in which one has mutually compelling but also conflicting associated duties. These are ubiquitous in the practice of law; examples include representing a client in a lawsuit against a former client. The former client may have revealed confidential information at the time that you can now use against him. If you do, you've violated your duty of confidentiality; if you don't, you may not be zealously representing the current client's interests. Law firms must keep extensive records precisely so as to avoid these kinds of conflicts. Some firms give clients the option of signing an exempting waiver, while others simply decline all associated cases.

Similar conflicts exist with faculty who have grading responsibility for a family member or romantic partner, health-care professionals who treat family members, and therapists counseling family or close friends. The lines here are no doubt fuzzy. Some professionals can be more objective with a relatively removed family member than, say, with a mentor. (The film *Wit* has a squirm-inducing scene in which a professor is given an intimate examination by a former student.) As before, the key response lies in being cognizant of the potential for conflict, striving to avoid taking on a conflicting duty, and working to shift decision-making authority to another when necessary.

A third type of conflict, less frequently discussed, is conflict of bias. The concern here is that the professional has particular prejudices – typically, but not always, irrational and unwarranted – that prevent her from acting in her client's best interest (Meyers, 1999). Imagine, for example, a deeply homophobic architect helping a gay couple design their dream home, or a surgeon who is an adamant atheist treating a Jehovah's Witness. Importantly, "bias" is a morally neutral term, so the concern here is the impact from *irrational* and *arbitrary* bias. One is rationally biased, for example, if one wants commercial jet pilots to be properly trained, but irrationally (and thus immorally) biased if one also wants them to be of a particular religious faith, since one's religious beliefs have no bearing on flying skills. Many, even most, biases reside below the level of explicit awareness and professionals must thus endeavor to be sufficiently self-reflective to recognize them and their impact on attitudes and behavior. Bias, when it is irrational and arbitrary, will almost certainly make it harder for the professional to fulfill her core normative duty of acting in the client's best interest.

The key to managing conflicts of bias is, first and foremost, to be sufficiently self-reflective to be aware of them, especially subtle ones. There are various mechanisms for detecting one's biases: Does a professor (or teacher) call upon men (or boys) more than women (or girls) in class? Does a lawyer or therapist interrupt one group of people more frequently? Does the cardiologist tend to dismiss women's chest pain as mere anxiety? Does the dentist shy away from treating known homosexuals?

Because such biases reside below the surface, it is especially important for the ethical professional to rely on a trusted friend or colleague to act as a sounding board. Having them alert one to seeming discrepancies can make all the difference in the achievement of ethically sound professionalism.

Other types of inducements, ones that do not neatly fit in these three categories, can also directly impact judgment and create perception problems. Among these are sexual attraction, let alone sexual offers, close friendships, and even distaste for certain personality types. Each can profoundly alter judgment or, at a minimum, create problems of perception. The mental health professions have long recognized these problems and are, thus, sticklers for maintaining "boundaries" precisely because they recognize just how judgment damaging these interpersonal factors can be.

In short, conflicts of interest can present themselves in an array of ways, so many that it is not realistic to expect professionals to successfully avoid them all; rather, the goal, in many cases, is to better manage them. This is all the more telling, in fact, when the conflicts are *structural*, part of the activity's foundations.

───────── ## 7.3 Structural Conflict of Interest ─────────

All the conflicts described above involve micro-level interactions, situations in which one's judgment is potentially altered because of a specific action, person, or relationship.[3] Some conflicts, however, are built into the very nature of the professional activity; that is, they cannot be avoided, but only managed, in better or worse ways.

They are *structural* because they are part of the defining features of the activity; one cannot engage in that activity as a professional without partaking of them. They are *conflicts* because those features naturally include both potentially damaging material inducements (e.g., basic compensation) and multiple and sometimes conflicting role-based duties.

Consider, for example, fee-for-service professional activities. The professional is quite rightly compensated based on the services provided. That compensation model, however, carries a built-in incentive to provide more services – so as to make more money – even if those services are not necessarily in the client's best interest. An oft-repeated joke version of this is that a therapist will make sure that you are sufficiently "crazy" to guarantee multiple visits, also ensuring that your "craziness" fits a category, per the *Diagnostic Statistical Manual*, that warrants reimbursement by the insurance company. Similar jokes can be told about lawyers extending cases and surgeons operating. They are jokes, but, as with most such humor, there is enough truth to them to make them resonate.

7.3.1 Universally present

Again, that these inducements are built into the nature of the activity does not mean that all, or even most, professionals' judgment is necessarily altered. Unlike, however, the more typical one-off nature of micro-level cases, when conflicts are structural, they are *always* present, because, again, they are part of the nature of the activity. Their pervasive presence also makes it harder for the client to determine whether his professional is in fact making choices in his best interest.

Sue Fisher, for instance, found that surgeons recommended surgical intervention – hysterectomies – for women who had insurance far more often than for women who presented with similar symptoms but did not have insurance (Fisher, 1988). When Fisher later interviewed the patients, she found that they had no idea that money had played a role in their health treatment and, more tellingly, nor did the professionals! Only when it was pointed out to them did some of those professionals realize how the inducement might have altered their judgment.

7.3.2 Roles and conflict of interest

Similar structural conflicts exist with role-based duties; managed health-care insurance programs are an oft-cited example. Participating physicians are duty bound by contract and commitment to fulfill the cost-containing efforts of the company, while also being duty bound to recommend treatment plans that would be of greatest benefit to their patients. Each of these duties is morally sound on its own – one should, of course, honor one's promises and, as we have seen throughout this book, professionals have a primary moral commitment to their client's well-being. The structural element here is not that the respective duties are necessarily in tension with each other; it is certainly possible that a managed care system can also prioritize client well-being. The problem is that in the *real* world where these plans exist – where physicians work and patients seek good medical care – they *do* conflict (Meyers, 1999). Thus the physician is in a bind: either duty that she prioritizes means at least a potential violation of the other.

7.3.3   Bias and conflict of interest

There are also structural conflicts of *bias*. Clinical ethics consultants, for example, particularly those who are in relatively tenuous employment circumstances, have an incentive to see ethics problems everywhere; without them, why would the hospital need their services? This creates a structural bias toward the prevalence of ethics conflict, a bias reinforced by ethicists being typically called upon in *hard* cases, ones that are rife with ethical concerns. These experiences create a subtle bias that alters the way ethicists view health care and thus how they view what is at work in specific cases. And, because subtle bias generally resides below the surface of self-awareness, it becomes particularly difficult for ethicists to fulfill their role of independent seekers of the best ethical solution.

Persons in law enforcement and criminal justice become similarly jaded. Most of the clients who end up in that system *have* broken the law, making it all too easy to see all clients as guilty of *something*. This is one reason that defense attorneys almost universally want a jury trial; they know that the lens through which judges view cases is colored by their long experience of watching criminals pass through their courtroom. In reality, such bias makes it very hard for judges to be able to wholeheartedly embrace the dictum "innocent until proven guilty" – even the very best, most compassionate judges who are most committed to justice.

7.3.4   Managing structural conflict of interest

Is there any way to avoid these structural conflicts? Not really. Professionals must be paid; they must establish practice-related relationships with a range of people who will have competing interests; and their typically repetitive experiences will produce subtle biases. Retainer arrangements or basic employment contracts alleviate some of the problem, but they also have their own structural conflict. If you agree, for instance, to compensate your attorney a set amount to handle a legal problem, he will have an intrinsic incentive to do less work on your case, saving time for other cases. Furthermore, not all professional relationships can be arranged around retainers and not all clients can afford to commit to often hefty up-front fees, and experience, whether repetitive or varied, is of course vital to the wisdom and judgment needed to be a good professional.

A last point, one that will re-emerge in the Epilogue: As professions have become more business conscious and, in particular, as practice choices are increasingly being made by persons other than the primary professional – for example, "utilization review" accountants – the structural conflicts have become correspondingly more embedded.

This characterization of the ubiquity of structural conflicts should not be read as pessimistically as it may appear. Professionals have been embedded in these conflicts for as long as there have been professions. Yet the vast majority of professional–client relationships are ethically sound, even ethically ideal. They are so because individual professionals have embraced the normative foundation of client well-being and that commitment is reinforced via systemic self-regulatory processes, including, where necessary, negative sanction.

Notably, these structural problems are not part of the *logic* of medicine, or lawyering, or any of the professions. One could theoretically provide medical service to a client without conflicting inducements or obligations – and do it for free out of the goodness of one's heart. Their existence is, however, endemic in any reality where services cost money and require corresponding commitments to a range of people and organizations. In short, they are endemic in our world.

The goal, therefore, must be to *manage* the conflicts in the best manner possible. This means, first, that those who deny the existence of these conflicts are also those whose judgment is most likely to be damaged (Katz et al., 2003). Thus, once again, the vital need for critical self-reflective awareness. Education helps in this, but professionals must also directly embrace the reality of the problem; it must become part of their professional culture; and that culture must be explicitly incorporated into professional self-regulating processes. Last, a key message of this book has been that the best professionals are also persons of strong moral character. Such persons are, by definition, critically self-aware and committed both to resisting inappropriate inducements and to better managing conflicts of obligation and bias.

7.4   Cases

7.4.1   Accepting a gift

One of your department colleagues has fallen ill about halfway through the term and the dean has asked you to take over the class. You already have a full load and it is a night section, but you are in the best position to pick it up mid-stream. And clearly the university has a responsibility to come up with some solution; the students cannot just be left hanging.

You agree (with promises for a course reduction down the road) and it turns out to be a great class. The students are on average quite a bit older and most have full-time jobs during the day; they are taking the course because they really want to learn, not just to jump through an academic hoop. They also recognize the sacrifice you are making and their appreciation has translated into a great partnership where everyone is working closely together to make it a valuable learning experience.

On the night of the final exam you are in your office hours when one of the better students pops in carrying a large box of asparagus! You know that he is a manager for a local farming company and he says to you, "Good evening Dr. Smith. I just wanted to tell you how grateful I am, we all are, that you were willing to take over the class. It's been great – a lot of fun and I really feel like I learned the material. I recall that you made a joke a couple of weeks ago about how much you like asparagus but, as a poor assistant professor, cannot afford it. I hope you will accept this in appreciation for all you've done."

This student has a solid A going into the final and, unless something strange happens, will assuredly earn that grade for the term. Further, to your best judgment he is wholly sincere. He is not trying to bribe you. He just wants to say thank you.

While you have been talking, you have also noticed that your colleague across the hall has come in and has his door open, and three of your students from another class are now waiting in the hall outside your door.

What should you do?

7.4.2 What now?

You are a well-respected attorney practicing exclusively in corporate law. Two of your friends, Jill and Sam, have decided to join forces to create a single criminal defense firm. They both worked with you many years ago and left, about two years apart, to form their own respective practices. You have long admired them both for their skills and professional commitment and see this as a great move for them and for their future clients.

They ask you if you will take care of the legal work of putting together the new company. They insist on paying your standard rate, but you refuse, saying that you will happily do it for expenses only.

All goes well – you have received all the material you need from each, including existing debts and assets. Somewhat to your surprise, Jill's practice has quite a bit more equity than Sam's and her existing client list is much longer, including some lucrative retainer arrangements with some of the wealthier families in town (whose adult children are famous for getting into legal trouble). But surely Jill and Sam have discussed all this, you muse, and you continue finalizing all the needed documents.

The next morning Sam comes rushing into your office, sweaty and out of breath. He has just learned that his wife, Jennifer, has been involved in a romantic relationship with Jill for well over a year.

He declares that "of course" he wants to dissolve any pending business partnership and to sue her for breach of trust. "I want to take her for everything she owns," he exclaims. You get him a cup of coffee and walk him to your conference room, telling him to wait while you make a few calls.

You quickly reach Jill and, sure enough, she happily admits to the affair. "I always assumed that Sam knew!" she says. "It's not like Jennifer and I have been all that discreet. And everyone knows Sam has been sleeping with MaryBeth – hell, they're practically living together." You get over your shock – evidently "everyone" didn't include you – and tell Jill that Sam is threatening to sue her and certainly wants to end any talk of a combined firm. She responds, "Well, that's just silly. Surely we're not going to let petty personal stuff get in the way of a great business arrangement?"

Sam, not surprisingly, declares there is nothing "silly" about this and he is all the more adamant now that he wants to file the lawsuit: "The sooner the better. And you will of course represent me, right?"

What should you do?

7.4.3 Treating everyone equally

You have worked like a dog throughout college, medical school, and residency to become an emergency room physician. You earned top grades and the accolades of your faculty at each step along the way. You accept a position at an inner city hospital and are similarly earning the respect of your new colleagues, both for your skills and for your dedication.

Part of your motivation to work in the emergency room was that your brother was a rookie police officer when he was shot and killed by a neo-Nazi gang member. When captured, the shooter declared that he had been "hunting Jewish cops and I just got lucky that I was able to get him." You vowed you would honor your brother's life by doing all you could to save the lives of other victims of such senseless violence.

You are on call on a Saturday night when word comes in that two rival gangs have just had a major shoot-out and that you should expect multiple gunshot victims any minute. Sure enough, the ambulances start arriving, triage is completed, and everyone who can possibly help is quickly assigned a patient.

Your first case is a young man with several major wounds to his legs and arms. He also has what appears to be a grazing injury to his lower abdomen. Feeling comfortable that it is nothing serious, you turn your attention back to the extremities and start patching him up – essentially prepping him for more extensive surgery. The patient has been conscious throughout and, between groans and pain outbursts, has been thanking everyone in sight for their efforts to save him. Eventually he passes out; you are somewhat surprised since the wounds do not look that severe and you have not administered any sedative. But you are also grateful: an unconscious patient is easier to work on.

Once you are confident that his extremity wounds are stabilized, you cut off what's left of his jacket and shirt to better assess the abdominal wound. And there it is: tattooed across most of his chest, a large swastika. You recoil in shock, an action the nurses and medical students all observe. At the same time, you realize that the wound is considerably more severe than you had judged: what you had thought was a graze is in fact any entry wound, just above his right kidney. You turn him back over but cannot find an exit wound and realize why he passed out: he is bleeding internally and, without immediate action, will likely die.

You find yourself choking down vomit and your hands shake as you pick up your instruments. What should you do?

NOTES

1. Davis's work on conflict of interest is among the most valuable in the field and my approach is largely informed by his analyses. See also Davis (1982, 1993, and 2001).

2. Despite the many strict federal conflict of interest requirements, there are two key – some would say glaring – exceptions. The US Supreme Court and the presidency. Individual justices have the final say on whether they should recuse themselves in particular cases and the president has no legal requirement to divest herself from economic activities that might serve to bias decision making inappropriately.

3. Many of the ideas and some of the text in this section derive from Meyers (2007).

REFERENCES

Brennan, T.A., Rothman, D.J., Blank, L., et al. 2006. "Health Industry Practices that Create Conflicts of Interest: A Policy Proposal for Academic Medical Centers." *Journal of the American Medical Association* 295 (4): 429–433.

Brody, Howard. 2005. "The Company We Keep: Why Physicians Should Refuse to See Pharmaceutical Representatives." *Annals of Family Medicine* 3 (1): 82–85.

Davis, Michael. 1982. "Conflict of Interest." *Business and Professional Ethics Journal* 1 (3): 17–27.

Davis, Michael. 1993. "Conflict of Interest Revisited." *Business and Professional Ethics Journal* 12 (4): 21–41.

Davis, Michael. 2001. "Introduction." In *Conflict of Interest in the Professions*, edited by Michael Davis and Andrew Stark, 3–21. New York: Oxford University Press.

Davis, Michael. 2005. "Conflict of Interest: A Primer." Paper presented at the annual meeting of the Association for Practical and Professional Ethics, San Antonio, Texas.

Elliott, Carl. 2004. "Pharma Goes to the Laundry: Public Relations and the Business of Medical Education." *Hastings Center Report* 34 (5): 18–23.

Fisher, Sue. 1988. *In the Patient's Best Interest: Women and the Politics of Medical Decisions*. New Brunswick, NJ: Rutgers University Press.

Katz, Dana, Caplan, Arthur L., and Merz, Jon F. 2003. "All Gifts Large and Small: Toward an Understanding of the Ethics of Pharmaceutical Industry Gift-Giving." *American Journal of Bioethics* 3 (3): 39–46.

Meyers, Christopher. 1999. "Managed Care Ethics: Anything New?" *Journal of Medical Ethics* 25 (5): 382–287.

Meyers, Christopher. 2004. "Institutional Culture and Individual Behavior: Creating an Ethical Environment." *Journal of Science and Engineering Ethics* 10 (3): 269–276.

Meyers, Christopher. 2007. "Clinical Ethics Consulting and Conflicts of Interest: Structurally Intertwined." *Hastings Center Report* 37 (2): 32–40.

Mower, Deborah S. 2014. "Reflections on a Culture of Sensitivity." *Teaching Ethics* 15 (2): 227–244.

New York Times. 2004. *Ethical Journalism: A Handbook of Values and Practices for the News and Editorial Departments.* http://www.nytco.com/wp-content/uploads/NYT_Ethical_Journalism_0904-1.pdf, accessed August 24, 2017.

US Office of Government Ethics. 2017. "Gifts from Outside Sources." https://www.oge.gov/Web/OGE.nsf/Resources/Gifts+from+Outside+Sources, accessed August 24, 2017.

Werhane, Patricia. 1999. *Moral Imagination and Management Decision Making.* New York: Oxford University Press.

Zimbardo, Philip. 2008. *The Lucifer Effect: Understanding How Good People Turn Evil.* New York: Random House.

8 Fidelity, Honesty, and Role-Based Duties

8.1   Promises   148

8.2   Honesty   150

8.3   Cases   156

      Notes   160

      References   161

It was the moment of truth, after which
they all got back to lying.

The Professional Ethics Toolkit, First Edition. Christopher Meyers.
© 2018 John Wiley & Sons Ltd. Published 2018 by John Wiley & Sons Ltd.

At the center of so much of ethics, law, and religion, fidelity is among the most fundamental of moral principles, particularly as expressed through promise keeping. To be faithful is to be honest, to adhere to vows, to honor contracts, to embrace covenants, and to accept a greater duty to those with whom we have a faithful relationship. Fidelity grounds trust and it makes for better and more secure social structures. And those who routinely violate it reveal themselves to be of vicious character, the sort most persons seek to avoid. By contrast, the expression "His word is his bond" is considered high praise of someone's character.

All persons, as we saw in Chapter 2, have a duty to fulfill generalized duties; but, as we have seen in various ways in this book, one's *role* as a professional (and as a friend, a partner, or a parent) carries with it a more stringent commitment to specific duties that are particularly relevant to that activity. One cannot, for example, fulfill one's role as a lawyer without scrupulously embracing confidentiality, or as a physician without committing to do no harm first and above all else. Fidelity is among the most basic of role-based professional duties – and is present in nearly all professional contexts – because of the foundational role trust plays in professional–client relationships.

As we saw in the earlier comparison between Kant and Ross (in Chapter 2), however, the practicalities of ethical life reveal that even such a basic principle as promise keeping cannot be an absolute. Life's contingencies sometimes place us in circumstances in which the most sincere promise must be violated on behalf of another important moral good. (Recall, from Chapter 2, the choice between stopping to help an accident victim and keeping a promise to meet a friend for coffee.)

Furthermore, trust is a tricky notion. Would you have greater trust in someone who blindly adheres to each and every promise, no matter how trivial, or in someone who relies on good judgment and wisdom to determine that, per the same example, the greater moral duty lies in stopping to help an accident victim than in keeping a promise to meet a friend for coffee? Or, worse, would you trust someone who insists on honesty to the point of cruelty, rather than *ever* deceiving someone?

This chapter will explore all these ideas by discussing the various elements of fidelity, with particular emphasis on the complexity of truthfulness and honesty and the associated professional role-based duties. As always, we shall conclude with cases that hone in on those duties while also revealing the vital role of practical wisdom in professional ethics reasoning.

8.1   Promises

Promise keeping, one of the simplest of concepts (if you commit to do something, you do it), is also among the most morally stringent, both because it has such powerful intuitive appeal and because so much of human sociality depends on being able to count on promised commitments. Indeed, the most popular and successful systems of political governance – social contract systems – are built upon at least implied promise. Citizens in the United States, for example, agree, at least implicitly, to abide by the Constitution, along with various state and local laws. This is exemplified in something as simple as the lines on a road: we trust that other drivers will stay on their side of the yellow lines, even as we zip past one another at 70 miles per hour.

As John Locke observed in his classic seventeenth-century discussion of civil society, the *Second Treatise of Government* (Locke, 1690), without such trust in one another and in a legal structure that defines and reinforces laws, citizens are more likely to revert to their baser impulses, particularly with respect to retribution, to the ultimate detriment of all. Thus persons – again, at least implicitly – agree to concede some of their natural rights, like individually punishing others who have transgressed against them, in exchange for greater security and stability (Locke, 1690).

The fidelity-based trust that makes for more civil society applies all the more vitally in personal and professional relationships. As noted throughout this book, it is the glue that holds such relationships together. If you couldn't trust a person's word about why they are doing it, think about how scary it would be to have them approach you with a sharp scalpel, or build a bridge, or dig around in your computer data, or represent you in a legal proceeding.

8.1.1   Moral foundations

Although they are typically associated with deontological theories, promises are also essential to aggregate utility – social structures collapse without the ability to rely on, for example, contracts – and to the development and maintenance of virtuous character.

Given this powerful moral place, can we not just base a whole model of professional ethics on promise keeping? If only moral life were so simple. Here are some of the associated problems. First, promises are often made too casually, causing the commitment to conflict with too wide a range of competing moral considerations. Take our exemplar case: should one in fact promise to meet someone at a particular time and place? Kant argued powerfully that since "ought" implies "can," we should only make promises about things over which we have complete or near-complete control. Thus one can promise to *try* to meet another or to do so unless something more morally compelling or out of one's control emerges. But the more qualifiers one adds the less compelling the promise seems. Imagine marriage vows that read: "I promise to be faithful unless something more morally compelling or outside my control emerges."

Second, persons also sometimes make careful promises about things they believe are in their control but in fact are not. "I promise to love you forever" is paradigmatic. One can legitimately promise not to cheat or abuse. One can also promise to provide financial support (though, of course, not a particular amount) and to maintain a supportive relationship with one's partner and children. But one cannot promise that the *emotions* one feels now will be present in ten, twenty, or thirty years' time.

Third, even if we could restrict promises to choices over which we do have complete control, what happens when competing promises conflict? This is precisely the problem of conflicting principles discussed in Chapter 2 (especially section 2.6): What should an engineer do, for example, when her promise to prioritize public safety conflicts with promises to the firm for cost containment? Or what should a physician do, when his commitment to prioritize his patient's needs conflicts with his managed care contract?

Fourth, there are, of course, cases in which an otherwise perfectly reasonable promise conflicts with another moral principle. A routinely cited version is where a friend loans you a pistol on your promise that you will give it back upon request. The friend shows up one day full of rage, having discovered his spouse in bed with someone else. He demands that you give him the gun. You resist, for obvious reasons, but he proclaims, "You promised!" The result is a clear conflict – a dilemma – between fidelity and non-maleficence, in which (based on the limited information provided) non-maleficence plainly should prevail. Similarly, the "buried bodies" case from Chapter 6 (section 6.4.2) creates at least a serious challenge to the promise of confidentiality, given its conflict with the principles of justice and beneficence.

In short, important as promises are, they are like all moral principles in that they must sometimes be balanced against competing moral considerations – including other promises.

8.2   Honesty

It would again appear that, with honesty, we have a seemingly simple and straightforward moral duty: it is wrong to lie to others. Easy enough, right?

Well, the first problem is in determining just what it *means* to lie. If you are considering buying a car from me but do not ask the right question – "How's the car's transmission?" – do I lie by not telling you that the gears are shot? What about if the grocery clerk gives you too much change? Is it dishonest to keep it, especially since it so happens that you were short-changed there just last week? And what about so-called white lies? Are they *really* lies?

As with most important moral concepts, determining the role that honesty should play in our lives is a two-step process. First, how do we best *define* the relevant concept and, second, what moral *value* does it have, especially when weighed against other moral considerations?

On the definitional question, we must first recognize that truth and falsity are not the only considerations. One can be unknowingly mistaken about the facts of a matter and, in communicating that information, one is mistaken but one is not dishonest. If I believe that there are unicorns on the dark side of Pluto and tell you all about them, I am not lying. I may be ignorant, stupid, naive, or even mentally disturbed but, as long as I genuinely believe this to be a true claim, I am *not lying*.

A silly case like this raises a tough definitional nuance. Assume that I really do not know there are not unicorns on Pluto, but *shouldn't* I know this? If I am going to make truth claims or, worse, violently act upon my beliefs, do I not have a responsibility to have done at least some research? To take a recent disturbing example, if I read on Facebook (as was reported during the presidential election campaign) that a Washington, DC, pizza joint is merely a front for Hillary Clinton's child sex ring, surely I have a duty to investigate the validity of such claims before entering the shop with an assault rifle?

This turns out to be a tremendously difficult question, since working to determine the accuracy of all of our beliefs could be a full-time job. There are also social niceties at work. No one particularly likes someone who constantly points out others' inaccuracies. Still, when persons engage in *willful* ignorance and convey such ignorance to others who might actually believe it, if it is not considered outright unethical behavior, their character will at least be called into question. And the more important the issue the more problematic and the more dishonest is the behavior.[1]

8.2.1   Professionals' duty to be informed

For professionals dealing with, by definition, vital concerns, willful ignorance over matters that impact their clients is fundamentally irresponsible. Even *negligent* ignorance – where the professional could easily enough obtain accurate information – is dishonest and unethical. When one accepts the professional role, with its potential for great good or harm, one thereby accepts the special duty to take reasonable steps to acquire accurate information; doing so is part of the very definition of being a knowledgeable and skilled expert.

Think of it this way. If I'm just Joe Schlub, beer chatting with my buds about unicorns and planets, I have no special duty to get it right. But what if I am an astronomer or a biology professor? Don't those roles carry a clear obligation to have accurate information about such unicorns?[2] What of a government teacher who claims that President Obama was not a US citizen? Or an environmental scientist who is a climate change denier? Again, when we inhabit life roles, and especially when we do so voluntarily, we take on the special obligations attached to that position. As we have been discussing throughout the book, this is particularly true for professionals, given the power they have to wreak great harm or to achieve great benefit for their clients.

Among the most vital of those special duties is the requirement to be sufficiently knowledgeable in one's field. A surgeon who does not, when he reasonably could, keep up with latest techniques, or a lawyer who does not, when she reasonably could, stay current with case law, or a software engineer who does not, when he reasonably could, learn a great new programming language, is being dishonest with his or her client (among likely other ethical failures) when his or her ignorance results in important information being excluded from the associated services.

The "reasonably could" caveat makes all the difference, of course, and there is no cookie-cutter answer for how to define it. More often than not the answer will come down to what one's colleagues do. In medicine, for example, malpractice claims are often decided by whether a jury believes that vital information was readily accessible, with "readily" determined by local practice standards.

8.2.2   Commission versus omission

One tactic for addressing these difficulties has been to rely upon the distinction between lies of *commission* and of *omission*. Lies of commission are those where one explicitly and knowingly communicates a falsehood, particularly in response to a direct question. These are thought to be worse, because of the explicit intent, than lies of omission where one simply does not volunteer information that another would find relevant.

In part because those lines are often very fuzzy, and because she believes that the distinction is ultimately irrelevant, Sissela Bok provides what I take to be the decisive analysis of dishonesty (Bok, 1999), that to be dishonest is to knowingly communicate in a way that results in others believing information one knows to be false. Such communications can be active and overt or passive and covert. They can also be made maliciously with the goal of hurting another, merely out of self-interest, or with good intent ("white lies" – which aiming to protect or even benefit another). None of this, Bok argues, matters to the *definition* of lying. All that counts is whether what one communicates results in someone believing something to be true that you know to be false, including questions of "*should* know," per the above analysis.

Furthermore, on this type of account all lies are prima facie wrong. All else being equal, one has a duty to be honest. As we saw in Chapter 2, however, it is rarely the case that all else *is* equal; sometimes the harms caused by being honest are far outweighed by the promotion of other principles or by the achievement of aggregate good.

8.2.3   Honesty and wisdom

Again, as discussed in Chapter 2, practical wisdom plays a crucial role in figuring out that balance. Whereas those who are consistently dishonest (typically for self-interested reasons) are rightly judged to be of low character, the person who is fundamentally honest but who also, on rare occasions, determines that dishonesty, or at least *softened* honesty, is the more ethical course is worthy of esteem. As Rosalind Hursthouse notes in her critique of blind obedience to rules and principles, key virtues are at stake on both sides: "[unreflective] honesty points to telling the hurtful truth, kindness and compassion to remaining silent or even lying" (2013, 649).

You can think of examples easily enough where blunt honesty is obviously the unethical course: "Do these pants make me look fat?" "Are you free for dinner Saturday night?" "Isn't my grandchild just the cutest you've ever seen?" Practical wisdom shows us that it is possible to retain the spirit of Bok's definition without being cruel: "I like the green ones on you a lot more"; "We have no plans, but it's been too long since Bill and I have had alone time, so I will have to beg off. Can I get back with you on another date?" "He certainly is adorable – I just love *all* babies!" You get the point. Ethical communication sometimes demands nuanced language.

8.2.4   Balancing duties

But what of harder cases, where the only way to achieve a moral good is through clear deception? One commonly cited conflict is whether physicians should lie to insurance companies – typically by providing a dishonest diagnosis that is covered rather than an honest one that is not (Tavaglione and Hurst, 2012). Taken more broadly, should professionals, in whatever field, act as advocates for their clients by fudging the truth in order to get around what they take to be irrationally bureaucratic rules? The "all lies are prima facie wrong" starting point reminds us that, for any such dishonesty to be justified, a carefully reasoned evaluation must take place, bringing in competing principles, aggregate utility, and character considerations. One cannot just casually assume that the good obviously outweighs the bad.

I routinely challenge my students to reflect upon how seriously they embrace honesty requirements. It is, after all, very easy to tell a small lie rather than to deal with the unpleasant or difficult ramifications of being honest. Or even to tell a big one if it means significant personal benefit or profit. To test them I gave them an exercise. They were to keep track of all their deceptive communications in a given forty-eight-hour period, to count how many there were, and also to pay attention to *why* they were dishonest: was it out of laziness, self-interest, malice, or to protect someone? Many students, it turned out, were pretty shocked by the sheer number of lies they tell. But they probably should not be. Our culture is imbued with various forms of fun and playful deceptions (Santa Claus, Easter Bunny, surprise parties). Further, most people just assume that politicians lie and that advertising is intentionally deceptive and these assumptions lead to the widespread belief that *caveat emptor* should still the norm in business dealings. Said differently, though we might claim that "honesty is the best policy," much of daily life practices include considerable deception.

8.2.5 Honesty and roles

Professionals, however, simply cannot afford to be perceived in such ways. They must be, and must be perceived to be, truthful, to be the sort of person who is at their core honest, even if on very rare occasions they engage in deception so as to benefit their clients. And note that only the latter reason is justified; laziness and self-interest cannot ethically enter into the calculation.

That said, roles again make a difference. Compare the honesty requirements of, respectively, judges, county prosecutors, and defense attorneys. The latter are expected, even sometimes ethically required, to be more deceptive, while the former can never be seen to lie (those practicing civil law fall somewhere in the middle). Physicians – and veterinarians and therapists – also routinely have to rely on the "nuanced language" referenced in section 8.2.3. Knowledgeable oncologists, for example, are aware that the term "cancer" often puts patients and families into a kind of mild shock, such that they sometimes do not really hear what follows – even if what follows is a very optimistic prognosis. Such physicians will thus often couch their assessments to patients and their families using terms like "growth" or "tumor," and filling in the specifics only later. On a strict reading of Bok's characterization, this language is at least temporarily dishonest. It is also, however, vital to effective communication and treatment and thus is almost certainly justified.

Hursthouse's critique of strictly rule-bound ethics theory (not surprisingly, her main target is Kant) is, I think, right. To be a person of character, to be a true professional, is to be deeply honest but not cruel. Sometimes, as she notes, kindness and compassion should prevail over strict allegiance to truth telling. But her position is also more ethically demanding. It is much harder to analyze and evaluate tough circumstances carefully, to determine how best to nuance language so as to retain a core truth, while also tempering it in a way that treats the recipient with respect and also promotes other important ethical concerns. And, circling back to promises, Hursthouse also stresses how practical wisdom teaches us to be circumspect in our promise making. Persons of character do not throw promises around like candy; rather, they save them for the things that really matter and over which they have as much control as possible.

Although these demands are greater for those in the caring professions, all professions, by definition, involve client interaction. For example, the more effectively an architect can translate "That's a really, really stupid idea; you are asking me to rewrite the laws of physics" into "Local zoning laws won't allow us to do that and, even if we could, it would push us way beyond your budget," the better she will be at working with her clients to achieve their mutually desired ends. Is it dishonest? Somewhat – she did not say what she was really thinking (that these are ding-bat clients who are going to be a handful). Is it more ethically appropriate? Almost certainly – she and they can now work together to achieve the goals of the relationship.

8.3   Cases

8.3.1   Committed to the company?

You are a structural engineer who has joined a new firm created by some college classmates. It is a small group but you are all very close. Everyone is starting new families, you spend holidays together, and you care deeply about one another's lives and well-being.

Everyone else was a year ahead of you in college and so you joined the company about six months after it had been formally created.

William, the company's president and your roommate for two years in college, recruited you pretty aggressively, flattering you in all the right ways and enticing you with an attractive salary and a small equity in the company. At the final interview you are about to shake hands on the employment deal when he says, "Sam, I do need you to really commit to this. You will be a key component in our future success and we can't afford to lose you and have to recruit all over again. Can you promise to do at least seven years with us?"

You saw this as very flattering – fresh out of school and already a key player in a great company, one where you can have a strong hand in developing its culture and future successes. You cannot imagine anything else being anywhere near as attractive and you happily shake hands on the deal.

You are now two years in and all is going really well. You love your work and your colleagues; you are like a family. Unfortunately, things are not quite so good on the home front. Your spouse feels stuck in a dead-end job, made worse by the fact that her parents have some health issues and she is having to drive an eight-hour round trip to their house on pretty much a weekly basis. You join her when you can, but work demands make that infrequent.

She has kept her ear to the ground for new opportunities and, sure enough, a great job – much better than her current one – has opened up in her parents' town and they have made it clear that it is hers if she wants it; they ask that she tell them by next week. To make things even more interesting, a structural design firm near there has also been reaching out to you and you are confident that the position is yours for the asking. It is a very good job in a large and very well-established firm. While it does not have some of the challenges and satisfactions that come with being a key player in a start-up, the pay and benefits are actually better and the housing costs are lower. Over dinner your wife makes it clear that she *really* wants to make the move. And you realize that you do too. It is a great opportunity, and you are aware of the toll those long drives are taking on your wife.

You grab some time with William the next day to tell him what you are thinking and he explodes: "Sam, you can't do this! We're right in the first phase of our biggest project ever – the project you almost single-handedly designed – and we simply cannot do it without you. And I assume I don't need to remind you of the promise you made to stay with us for seven years. If you leave, there's no telling what will happen to the company."

You point out that the seven-year agreement was never put in writing and he just shakes his head and says, "Sam, I trusted you. We're like family. I took your word to be your bond."

What should you do?

8.3.2 A contract is a contract

Imagine that you are a forty-six-year-old physician in the final stages of an acrimonious divorce. You are also a cancer survivor, having gone through aggressive chemotherapy for breast cancer. Knowing that the treatment is likely to make you infertile, you and your then husband cryogenically froze five embryos and you now want to use them to get pregnant … in spite of his adamant objections.

This is the position Dr. Mimi Lee recently found herself in.[3] Dr. Lee argued that this was the only chance she had to have a child of her own as time was running out. Her soon to be ex-husband, Stephen Findley, said that he did not want her raising his children if they were not together, but, more importantly, the contract they both signed when the embryos were frozen was explicit: both parties must agree to their future use and, if they cannot agree, particularly in the event of a divorce, the embryos will be destroyed.

The San Francisco Superior Court judge Anne-Christine Massullo was sympathetic to Dr. Lee's situation but sided with Findley, determining that binding agreements like this must prevail. (It helped Findley's case that the fertility clinic at the University of California, San Francisco, urged this outcome, arguing that their program depended on being able to promise that agreements would be respected in perpetuity.)

The case is in many ways a standard contract decision but also in many ways completely new, given that potential human life is at stake, as well as a person's ability to conceive and raise children. Many thus see it as a precedent-setting case, particularly if Dr. Lee successfully appeals Massullo's ruling.

Setting aside the legal details, do you think the judge made the right *ethical* decision? Be sure to include in your analysis such questions as the moral force of promises, the implications attached to the destruction of the embryos, and the impact on aggregate utility if the contract is voided.

8.3.3   The lying ethicist

Of all professionals, consulting ethicists must especially be seen as beyond ethical reproach: their very credibility is rooted in their character. If they are perceived to be dishonest, their recommendations and teaching will not be taken very seriously.

Imagine that you are a clinical ethicist working at a good-sized teaching hospital. You provide standard consulting services, including case evaluations and recommendations, education for the residents (and undergraduates from the local university), and policy development and implementation. You have a good relationship with nearly all the attending physicians and get along well with residents – many of whom regularly look to you for advice. They trust your judgment because they know that you have been doing this for many years and have a nuanced understanding of medical practice and of the ethical issues that regularly arise therein.

This morning you were doing ethics rounds in the intensive care unit, during which you had a challenging conversation with the unit's director over a young patient who was almost certainly dying from uncontrollable coccidiodal meningitis. He is a twenty-nine-year-old farmworker with a wife and three young children and undoubtedly picked up the fungus working in the fields. His condition is deteriorating rapidly but he is occasionally awake and able to converse with his treating team.

You asked the director if the patient knows he is dying. She responded, "I haven't told him that point blank, but surely he knows, based on everything else we've told him." You questioned that conclusion and asked whether he has a right to know. She was clearly struggling and answered, "He's so young. I just hate thinking there's nothing we can do about this. And there *is* a glimmer of hope, hope that will surely be wiped out if I tell him how bad it is. Let me sleep on it and we can talk more tomorrow." You agreed and told her how much you appreciated that she was taking it seriously.

As you routinely do, you stop by the patient's room, with your students in tow, just to make sure that he and his family don't have any concerns with which you might be able to help. You decided years ago that small kindnesses at times like these can make all the difference, especially to families. The patient is awake when you enter, but staring into space. You make the usual inquiries and after a couple of minor issues that you promise to try to get fixed, his wife starts to talk, pauses, and starts crying, and then asks, "Please, doctor, tell us whether he is going to get better. He's not going to die, is he?" Caught off guard – no patient or family member has ever asked you this before – you also notice that the patient turned his head to you at the question and is watching you intently.

You realize that you can lie and give them assurances – it certainly would be a kind and compassionate, if also decisively dishonest, response. Or you can deflect the question and say, "I'm really not in a position to answer that – you'll have to ask Dr. Jones." Or you can sit down, commit to the time to doing it right, and tell them the truth – knowing that, if you do, you will also likely be crushing any remaining hope. You also know that Dr. Jones will be furious with you if you usurp her position and tell them the truth.

What should you do?

NOTES

1. The prevalence of so-called "fake news" likely played a significant role in the 2016 US presidential election and, in many cases, involved exactly this abdication of duty to pursue the truth (Holan, 2016).
2. A related issue is whether biology teachers should accept the truth of evolution. An astonishing (to my mind) 13 percent of high school biology teachers advocate a creationist view (Welsh, 2011).

3. http://www.eastbaytimes.com/2015/11/18/judge-contract-trumps-
    womans-rights-in-s-f-frozen-embryo-fight, accessed August 25, 2017.

REFERENCES

Bok, Sissela. 1999. *Lying: Moral Choice in Public and Private Life.* New York:
    Vintage Books.
Holan, Angie Drobnic. 2016. "2016 Lie of the Year: Fake News." Politifact.
    http://www.politifact.com/truth-o-meter/article/2016/dec/13/2016-lie-
    year-fake-news, accessed August 25, 2017.
Hursthouse, Rosalind. 2013. "Normative Virtue Ethics." In *Normative Ethical
    Theory: An Anthology*, 2nd ed., edited by Roger Crisp, 645–651. Boston:
    John Wiley & Sons.
Locke, John. 1690. *Second Treatise of Government.* https://www.gutenberg.
    org/files/7370/7370-h/7370-h.htm, accessed August 25, 2017.
Tavaglione, Nicolas, and Hurst, Samia. 2012. "Why Physicians Ought to Lie
    for Their Patients." *American Journal of Bioethics* 12 (3): 3–14.
Welsh, Jennifer. 2011. "13% of H.S. Biology Teachers Advocate Creationism
    in Class." Live Science. http://www.livescience.com/11656-13-biology-
    teachers-advocate-creationism-class.html, accessed August 25, 2017.

9 Formal Justice, Bias, and Allocation of Resources

9.1	Arbitrary Features	163
9.2	The Complexity of Justice	165
9.3	Formal Justice	166
9.4	Bias	170
9.5	Distributive Justice	172
9.6	Cases	176
	Notes	180
	References	181

'Let's argue our case anyway.'

© Clay Bennett

The Professional Ethics Toolkit, First Edition. Christopher Meyers.
© 2018 John Wiley & Sons Ltd. Published 2018 by John Wiley & Sons Ltd.

In 2007 a lesbian couple, Sharolyn Takata and Donna Jones, took their nine-year-old daughter, who was suffering from a high fever, to the emergency room at San Joaquin Community Hospital (later renamed Adventist Health Bakersfield), in Bakersfield, California. At the hospital, Sharolyn, the biological mother, was allowed to accompany her daughter into the examination room but Donna was not. Told that safety and crowding concerns meant that only one visitor could accompany the child, the couple nonetheless noted that there were other patients with multiple visitors at the bedside. Not wanting to add to an already stressful situation, they decided that they would swap time, so that only one person was at the child's bedside at any given time. But even this plan failed: a security guard blocked Donna from entering at all (Hagedorn, 2007).

The hospital is part of Adventist Health, a hospital organization founded and run by the Seventh Day Adventists, a Christian sect that strongly opposes gay marriage. Despite this, and despite initial denials that discrimination was at work (a spokeswoman said that the decision was made at the charge nurse's discretion and was motivated by safety and confidentiality), the hospital eventually apologized to the couple and agreed to revise its policies and to train its staff on discrimination and bigotry.

But why? Why apologize and devote resources to training when the staff members appeared to be acting consistently with their founding church's tenets?

The decision to apologize was undoubtedly motivated in part by public relations and to avoid litigation. At the same time, the hospital also came to accept that what they did was *unjust*.[1] It was unjust because staff members allowed *arbitrary* factors – the couple's sexual orientation – to impact how they delivered health care to the family.

9.1   Arbitrary Features

Notice that saying the decision was unjust says nothing about the morality of homosexuality or of gay marriage. One can believe that homosexuality is a sin but still recognize that one's sexual orientation is irrelevant to best health-care practices, including, in this case, the loving support that a nine-year-old needs when she is very ill.

This point reinforces a key element of formal justice. Discrimination per se is not necessarily bigotry; for an act to qualify as discrimination, it must be *arbitrary* discrimination. In this case, sexual orientation was irrelevant to how the treating team needed to manage medical care; the only thing that mattered was that a sick child needed her parents' loving attention and that was denied.

However, contrast that decision with, say, a judgment to exclude gays and lesbians from Adventist *ministry*. Although you and I might disagree with the church's position on gays and lesbians, Adventists nonetheless have every legal and ethical right to develop (within parameters) their belief system and corresponding leadership choices. For them, one's sexual orientation is relevant to whether one can be a church leader and, if someone disagrees, they need not be members of that faith; communion as an Adventist is, after all, wholly voluntary. Hence, the church is, by definition, engaging in *discrimination*, but because it is not arbitrary it is not *unjust* discrimination; it is not bigotry.

Similar examples can be given for the discrimination we all regularly employ in hiring someone for a job. We select only those who are qualified, based on their training, skills, expertise, and even character traits. For that matter, faculty members also discriminate every time they grade, deciding that some papers or exams are worthy of higher or lower grades. Similarly, a surgery department discriminates rationally and justly when it insists that its department head be a surgeon, but discriminates irrationally when it also insists that the head be male. Training and skills are directly relevant to be the program leader; gender is wholly immaterial. But, by the same token, gender *could* be a rationally relevant consideration in some hiring choices, ones as trivial as whether a bathroom attendant is male or female, or as significant as the gender of the emergency room professional assisting with a rape evaluation.

We thus see an essential element of formal justice. While discrimination per se is morally neutral, *arbitrary* discrimination – discrimination based on factors that are not relevant to the choices or actions at hand – violates justice.

———————— **9.2 The Complexity of Justice** ————————

Given the professional's duty to act in the client's best interest, *whoever* that client is, justice is clearly among the most important of professional ethics principles. It is also among the most complex. In addition to the formal considerations noted above, justice also demands that we give careful ethical attention to how resources are allocated.[2] These latter considerations, usually categorized under distributive justice, are most pressing at the *macro* level. For example, how should governmental leaders allocate revenue to make sure that everyone has access to good-quality legal representation or health-care services?

Distributive justice concerns can also, as we shall see, find their way into micro-level professional–client encounters, but the typical professional will encounter questions of formal justice far more frequently. At the micro level the focus should be on making sure that only relevant features are present in professional–client interactions, while at the meso, institutional, level professionals have to give attention to whether hiring, promotion, and leadership choices are clear of any unjust discrimination, and at the macro, societal, level some professionals will also give attention to such concerns as whether and how undocumented members of the community receive social benefits like health care and education. All these justice-related choices also directly reveal individual professionals' *character*; those with more developed virtue will fully embrace the "whoever the client is" standard, while others will (often subconsciously) allow various degrees of bigotry to slip into their relationships and practices.

It is important to note that, of all the ethics principles under discussion in this book, justice is easily the most debated in the literature, with arguments going all the way back to Plato and Aristotle. We shall sidestep that debate here, in part through a division of justice into formal and distributive justice, treating them almost as separate principles, and in part by relying on the most common interpretations of each. We shall also focus primarily on how formal justice plays out in micro-level interaction, giving less attention to resource allocation questions. As always, we shall also explore cases to see how these concepts play out in practice.

9.3 Formal Justice

Consider for a moment the symbol that metaphorically stands for justice in the United States. Three key features stand out. First, she holds scales, striving to make sure that decisions are properly balanced; second, she holds a sword as an assurance that judgments will be swiftly applied and enforced; third, and most importantly, her eyes are covered so that she cannot see on whom her justice is being bestowed (she is blind to any associated arbitrary factors and therefore impartial).

Besides the obvious instance of the legal profession, how then, are these concerns relevant to professional ethics? The short answer is to repeat the earlier noted standard, that the professional's duty is to use her best skills and knowledge to further her clients' interests, ideally without any consideration of factors that are not demonstrably relevant to the service being provided. That is, she is to use her professional talents *objectively*.

9.3.1 Justice and objectivity

That said, and as we shall see in the bias discussion in section 9.4, strict objectivity is probably an unrealistic standard. Just as most journalists now recognize that the once revered "mirror on the world" model of objective reporting is not possible (Meyers, 2015), so also, for example, must self-aware faculty recognize that subtle bias will find its way into grading, at least wherever non-quantitative criteria like writing quality or strength of argument are part of the evaluation. Similar biases seep into all but the most virtuous of professional–client interactions, exactly as they do in all but the most virtuous of non-professional human relationships. In every-day interactions, such biases, disturbing though they may be, rarely cause significant harm. The nature and stakes of the professional–client encounter, by contrast, create far greater opportunity for unjust impacts. The ethical professional, thus, takes this into account and devises procedures to lessen those effects (e.g., many professors employ anonymous grading).

For *all* the professions, but especially for those providing direct treatment or other care, justice demands that particular attention be paid to whether one is handling clients with equal dignity and respect and making sure that irrelevant factors do not unduly influence one's work. Obviously, irrelevant factors include all the usual areas where humans struggle with various forms of bigotry: race, ethnicity, gender, sexual orientation, religion, age, culture, and disability. Subtler but still damaging forms of unjust discrimination relating to factors like economic standing, unpleasant appearance, body size, and even an unlikable personality may manifest themselves. It should be no surprise that professionals – just like everyone – generally find it more pleasant to work with smart, fun, charming, and good-looking people. And, again not surprisingly, if they find it more pleasant, they will be naturally (and most often subconsciously) inclined to engage with them more sympathetically and thoroughly.

9.3.2   Negative impacts

In contrast to those quality-enhancing features, professionals can be put off by, among other things, their annoyance or frustration with clients. For example, it is easy for a professional's patience to wear thin with so-called "frequent flyers." These include non-compliant patients who regularly need treatment – often fairly extensive treatment – for conditions that can be largely self-managed; repeat drug offenders; dental patients who do not engage in good mouth hygiene; and students who seem to have a crisis that prevents them from completing their work every term. Do such issues frustrate and annoy professionals to the point where they provide lower-quality service? Of course they do, unjust as that may be. That reaction is a natural human response, but one that ends up meaning that such clients receive reduced or lower-quality service.

To say that professionals are naturally attuned to such annoyances and must strive to keep them from resulting in an unjust service is not to say that justice always demands the *same* response. Building upon the compliance examples, while all patients must be treated with the same level of *quality*, particularly in emergency situations, it may be that the *type* of treatment can vary appropriately. For example, it may be necessary to develop (largely unenforceable) contracts with "frequent flyers," with the goal of motivating them to undertake lifestyle choices that other patients have already embraced. It may also mean recognizing that the best one can do for a homeless addict is to help them recover merely to the point where they can enjoy the very thing that is doing them harm (tobacco, drugs, alcohol), but it may also be the only thing that still gives them joy or pleasure.

9.3.3   Circumstantial responses

The need for different types of service was made clear to me early in my career as a clinical ethicist. During ethics rounds one day, internal medicine residents were voicing frustration over a patient with chronic obstructive pulmonary disease[3] who needed regular pulmonary "tune-ups" – typically a few days on a ventilator. And then, as soon as he was healthy enough to walk, he would step outside for a smoke. One of the residents, who had treated the patient on multiple occasions, voiced her frustration, "Enough already – if he wants to slowly kill himself I'm not going to get in his way."

The attending physician immediately barked: "Is he not a human? Is he not sick? Is it not your job to treat sick humans? Do you question the source of all your patients' diseases and refuse to treat those who are negligent in their health management? And when was the last time, by the way, that *you* went to the gym?" Without being consciously aware of it, this physician was delineating the principle of justice, noting that the resident, whose primary duty was to use her best knowledge and skills to treat her patients, was actually urging unequal, unjust treatment. The attending physician then went on to implicitly invoke the principle of beneficence by more quietly asking the residents to consider the patient's life, noting that a whole series of things must have gone terribly wrong for him to end up like this. "No one intentionally chooses to destroy their life in this fashion, so show him some sympathy. What else does he have in his life besides his booze and cigarettes? And, more importantly, do your duty and treat him to the best of your ability."

In this case, and given his history and life circumstances, "best treatment" meant getting him cleaned up enough that he could leave the hospital, where he would almost certainly continue his self-destructive behavior. With a patient who is better able to commit himself to health management, however, "best treatment" may include another day or two in the hospital to get more fully stabilized and likely an attempt to get him enrolled on a substance abuse program. Thus, while the type and extent of treatment may vary, as determined by their relative circumstances, as long as the *quality* is comparable (again, relative to circumstance), justice is not violated.

Note, however, that these discussions have focused on the micro level, on the immediate physician–patient relationship, with its grounding in the professional's primary duty to act on behalf of her client. Contrast this with the hospital's utilization review manager, whose duty is to act as a *gatekeeper*, striving to keep costs down.

He appropriately – and justly – has a duty to review, for example, the number of repeat visits and to suggest something like a health-care contract with non-compliant patients. "Appropriately" and "justly" because *his* client is the hospital and its shareholders (or taxpayers), not the immediate patient, just as those working on state or national health policy must approach issues from a macro perspective, relying, one would hope, on analyses rooted in principles of distributive justice.

9.4 Bias

As should be clear from the examples so far, the greatest threats to formal justice are not explicit and intentional violations but rather largely unintentional, even *unaware*, violations caused by often subconscious biases. Although society still has a considerable way to go, we certainly have made tremendous progress on *explicit* bigotry. It is now rare to hear persons overtly denigrate others on racial, ethnic, homophobic, or religious grounds.[4]

Covert bigotry is, of course, still rampant, which reveals that the underlying motivation is a subtler kind of bias (Halloway, 2014). As myriad examples of compelling research show (Mower, 2014), implicit bias is built into human interaction: we *all* have it. Normal communication, in fact, relies on a wide range of generally benign implicit biases – everything from the shorthand of ordinary language to what kinds of behavior we can expect of others on a four-lane freeway.

As Patricia Werhane explains, even our very *perceptions* are filtered through the bias of our respective conceptual schemes:

> We all perceive, frame, and interact with the world through a conceptual scheme modified by a set of perspectives or mental models. Putting the point metaphorically, we each run our "camera" of the world through certain selective mechanisms: intentions, interests, desires, points of view, or biases, all of which work as selective and restrictive filters. (Werhane, 1999, 49)

Some versions of this analysis suggest that we cannot help *but* see the world through such lenses, which dictate our understanding of the world and define our values within it (Zimbardo, 2008). However, even if that perspective is too pessimistic about our ability to rationally overcome our respective lenses, it would be foolish to think that they have *no* impact.

Said differently, these studies show persuasively that we all bring our biases into interpersonal encounters – including professional-client encounters. For example, physicians with implicit (but, again, often subconscious) gender biases will be more inclined to interpret women's potential cardiac issues as mere anxiety or hysteria (Chiaramonte and Friend, 2006). Similarly, teachers are likely to punish African American students more harshly than white students who have committed similar infractions (Okonofua and Eberhardt, 2015). And gays and lesbians, whether they are the accused or the victim, are more likely to face prejudice by jurors (Malik and Salerno, 2014). In each of these cases, persons are being treated differently and to their disadvantage because of arbitrary factors. That is, each such case represents a violation of formal justice.

9.4.1 Managing bias

Given that bias is universal and can result in violations of formal justice, and given that it often exists below the surface – both in individual consciousness and social awareness – there are two keys to being an ethical professional. First, and at the risk of redundancy, professionals must be *zealously self-reflective*. Do you treat your female (black, gay, etc.) clients differently? Are you quicker to dismiss their complaints or to reject their excuses? Are you as willing to go the extra step to help them achieve their goals?

Second, we all need a good editor, someone who can challenge our motivations and actions. Again, one of the lessons from analyses of journalism objectivity is that the best, most thorough coverage is *systemic*, where multiple eyes and perspectives are taken into account (Meyers, 2015). Professional bias works in the same way. The more we can rely on others from varying points of view to assess our attitudes and actions the more likely it is that unjust biases will at least be reduced.

─────────────── 9.5   Distributive Justice ───────────────

Imagine that it is 2009 and you have just been appointed provost of a state university in California. The state's budget analyst recently announced a $42 billion deficit for the coming year and the governor has stated that every state agency will take a major cut; your campus is looking at a 12 percent reduction. Having made all the non-vital cuts last year, you are left with only bad choices: lay-off of faculty and staff and possible cancellation of programs.

While constrained by a union contract that prioritizes a mix of seniority and rank, you still have a number of different ways in which you can approach the cuts. The approach your business officer is pushing is to go by strict economics: simply crunch the numbers and lay off those whose salaries are the highest. But you realize that included in this mix will be people who are close to retirement but need a few more years to get there. It will also cause disproportionate harm to some academic disciplines, that is, those that happen to have higher-paid faculty.

Another approach is to cut whole programs, focusing on those with fewer majors, and to lay off all the associated faculty. But you also know that those programs provide a disproportionate share of service classes (general education and major cognates). You also worry that this approach does not sufficiently account for the different circumstances of the relevant faculty: while some could retire easily enough, others are early career members with young families.

A third approach is simply to go after all the temporary faculty, those not in tenured or tenure stream positions. Some of these, you know, have full-time work outside campus and teach mainly to help the departments and students and to earn a few extra dollars; hence, these faculty members would not be badly harmed. But some have been dedicated members of the faculty for many years – decades even – and are a vital part of the campus's mission. Additionally, they generally earn less than tenured faculty, so you would have to let many more of them go. In short, you have no good options: your already too small pie just got a lot smaller and there are simply too many very good people and programs clamoring for a piece.

With variation in details, campus administrators (business owners, corporate human resource managers, etc.) across the country faced similar choices during the Great Recession. Some approached it cynically, using their budget-driven power to restructure the university to their liking. Others avoided the hard questions and simply used the meat cleaver of seniority: last hired, first fired, thereby ignoring any disproportionate harm caused by such a rule-bound approach.

Others, though, strove to make the cuts as *justly* as possible. Considerations of formal justice certainly played a role – they could not, for example, target women or minorities – but the primary questions were rooted in *distributive* justice: how to most *fairly* apportion scarce resources.

9.5.1 What is fair?

As noted, this turns out to be a tremendously difficult question, with answers ranging from the renowned Marxist credo "From those with greatest ability, to those with greatest need" to answers from a libertarian bent – distributions are just when, and only when, the rights of all those affected are respected (Nozick, 1974).

Given how hard these questions are, it is fortunate that most professionals do not have to address problems of distributive justice directly. In relation to the discussion, their primary duty is to look out for the well-being of their clients, leaving institutional (meso-level) and social (macro-level) questions to administrators, policy analysts, and legislators.

When, however, their work resides within organizational settings – for example, hospitals, universities, and district attorney or public defender offices – allocation decisions at that meso level will often directly impact the quality of their service: physicians will have to treat more patients, professors teach more students, and lawyers handle more cases. Some professionals, thus, become enthusiastic participants in "shared governance" processes, hoping to impact resulting decisions in a way that prioritizes client service or their program's needs.

The rub, though, is that becoming so engaged consumes what most professionals consider to be their most precious resource – *time*. It also distracts the professional from the very client service they are trying to preserve. For those, however, who do want to help resolve these thorny problems of resource allocation (or *must*, as in the case of professional administrators), one would hope that their deliberations are grounded in a model of just distribution.

9.5.2 Rawls's theory

As noted, there are any number of such models available in the literature, all powerful and all intricate and difficult (Dworkin, 2013; Nozick, 1974; Sandel, 1998; Walzer, 1984). Notably, all of these are, in one way or another, responses to John Rawls's classic, *A Theory of Justice* ([1971] 1999).

Rawls's very complex argument can be summarized as follows. In order for policies to be just, they must, first, respect persons' liberty; second, they must promote, to the extent possible, equality of opportunity to access social goods; and, third, they must distribute new resources in a way that creates the greatest advantage for the least well off. Let us take each in turn.

Policies are just only insofar as they successfully promote the greatest *liberty* for all affected. While on the surface this appears to be a deontological prioritization of liberty, there is also a strongly utilitarian quality. This would allow some restriction on individual liberty as long as in doing so overall aggregate utility is increased. An easy example is driving laws. Society justly limits our freedom to drive while under the influence of drink because it enhances others' liberty of transport; that is, others can freely use society's roads with a greatly reduced fear of accident.

Justice demands that all persons have an *equal chance* to access social goods such as wealth, education, and health care – essentially the conditions that contribute to a flourishing life. This means that when, through no fault of their own (so that merit or formal justice is not at play), persons are at a disadvantaged starting point, society should make amends to give them an equal chance to succeed. Affirmative action programs, for example, are based upon this principle.

In what is widely seen to be the most controversial of his conclusions, Rawls states that any rational person who does not know where they fall in society's hierarchies (being behind, in his language, "a veil of ignorance") would self-interestedly want the greatest advantage to go to the neediest, since that might very well include them. Importantly, the principle does not say that the most well off do not also benefit from these new resources, just that they benefit at a *proportionally* lower rate. Progressive tax models rely on a similar principle: society taxes billionaires so that new profit adds significantly to their wealth, but also so that society's least advantaged benefit even more, relative to *their* existing baseline. For example, a 10 percent increase for someone below the poverty line substantially improves their situation, but at a relatively low dollar amount. By comparison, if the billionaire's wealth is increased by only 5 percent (because they have been taxed for the difference), they still receive a tremendous absolute increase in the amount but with a limited improvement in their overall economic standing. Both are made better off, but the greater relative advantage goes to the neediest.

Applying these principles to the university cuts described earlier would mean rejecting any of the simplistic options, forcing instead a complicated and nuanced approach. The provost would have to take into account individual and program need, opportunity costs for students and faculty, and a determination of which choices best enhance aggregate liberty to pursue life's goals. Cuts would thus be rationally targeted: some senior faculty – those who can most afford to retire – would likely be laid off, along with part-timers, as long as those choices also align with a rational evaluation of student and programmatic opportunity needs.

In short, these analyses reinforce just how tremendously difficult problems of distributive justice can be. Does it mean that one should just punt and go with the easy formula: find a set of consistent rules and stick to them, regardless of the impact? Not if one is committed to achieving just solutions across all aspects of professional life.

Fortunately, and to repeat myself, the typical professional will rarely have to engage with such difficult questions. Rather, she will be in a reactive position: given the allocation decisions that others have made, how can she best benefit her client? Having some appreciation for Rawlsian and other principles of distributive justice will help her realize this, as will a basic commitment to achieving the best ethical outcomes and to expressing the highest possible character, which takes us back to careful ethics reasoning.

One last point before moving to cases. Although I have presented formal and distributive justice as essentially separate principles, they also regularly overlap. One cannot determine how best to promote equal opportunity, for example, without addressing whether it is sometimes acceptable to make choices based on otherwise arbitrary factors like race or gender. The overlap also emerges systemically via decisions about, for example, how to allocate scare county resources for legal services. In underfunding a public defender's office, accused criminals will more likely have their formal justice threatened.

9.6 Cases

9.6.1 Equal treatment for cheaters?

You are near the bottom of the stack of term papers for your professional ethics class when you realize that the current one is very similar to one that you graded a few hours ago. You dig that earlier one out and, sure enough, they are almost identical, with just a few phrasing changes here and there. You had actually scored the first one quite highly, giving it a B+. It was written by a woman named Elena who had regularly attended class and engaged in class discussions.

She had even come by the office last week to discuss the topic. By contrast, the second was written by Henry, who showed up only occasionally and often took off right after the daily quiz. When he did stick around, he sat in the back and spent most of his time with his eyes and thumbs glued to his mobile device.

Your academic dishonesty policy is clearly spelled out on the syllabus: any significant violation – and this certainly qualifies – will result in an F for the course and likely university discipline. Furthermore, you have a class contract in which everyone agrees to abide by the standards of honesty and justice laid out in the syllabus and reinforced in class conversations.

You email each student, asking them to come see you (separately). Elena responds within the hour and schedules an appointment for the next morning. Upon arrival, and before you can even challenge her, she blurts out, "I am so sorry, Professor. I didn't sleep a wink last night … I should never have let Henry borrow my paper. Even though he never flat out said he was going to copy it, I was pretty sure he would." You remind her of the plagiarism policy and the class contract and she says, "I know, I get it: I screwed up and deserve whatever punishment you think is appropriate." You tell her that you appreciate her taking responsibility now and explain that you need to talk to Henry and will consider your options. As she leaves, she adds, "If there are any possibilities here – I'm willing to rewrite the paper, do extra credit, take an exam showing I know the material – I'm there. And, if it matters, I really loved the class and learned a lot from it."

Henry, by contrast, finally responds after the third email, the one in which you state you will be giving him an F and reporting him to Student Conduct. He saunters in, thirty minutes late, and is immediately belligerent: "Why did you call me in? It's the break and the last thing I wanted to do was have to come see you." You explain what you found in the papers and he says, "Well, I guess she must've copied off me somehow." You ask how that could have happened and he replies, "Beats me – she must've snuck into my dorm room." You ask a few simple questions about the content and argument structure of the paper, but he responds, "Look, professor, that was a week ago. I can't remember any of it now."

It is clear both have violated the academic dishonesty policy and, per the guidelines set forth in it, both should receive an F. A strict application of formal justice would require that they be treated equally here: the fact that you like her more and that she's more respectful to you should be irrelevant.

Or should it? What is the just response for each?

9.6.2   Bias and just representation

Gary always hates Mondays. That is the day his case load invariably skyrockets, the result of the spike in arrests after a weekend of drunken criminal behavior. He has been in the Public Defender's office for only nine months and is already sending out his resumé – he thinks he just has to find other practice, maybe work for a church group or other non-profit organization. Surely there is a way, he muses, in which he can practice law in a manner consistent with his deep religious beliefs.

His shoulders sag as he picks up the stack of folders on the desk and starts working through them. The third is yet another assault case. Sam Jones was picked up outside a bar having beaten someone badly. A typical case, except he notes that the clerk has included a cryptic statement: "She is mid-transition." She?

Gary meets with Sam in the men's jail interview room later that morning and realizes what the statement meant: Sam is, from all appearances, a woman. Realizing that Sam is in the process of gender reassignment, Gary tries to hide his obvious disgust. Before he can begin his interview, though, Sam says, "You have to get me out of here: I'm not a man anymore. If I stay in here I'm going to be raped, or worse."

Calling herself "Samantha," she proceeds to explain that she was at a rough bar, admittedly looking to hook up with someone for the night. She connected with a guy and they started making out in the back alley when he realized that Samantha still has a penis – she had not yet undergone that phase of the transition. He cursed her, pulled a knife, and gave her a quick cut – she showed Gary where the slash on her arm had been treated – and she reacted in fear and anger. When it was all over he lay on the ground with a badly beaten face and a broken jaw.

Before he can catch himself, Gary asks, "What were you thinking, hitting on a guy in that way and in that bar?" In response, Samantha merely bows her head and starts crying. Part of Gary is thinking, "She deserves this. Maybe a week or two in this jail will straighten her – him! – out." But he also realizes that he has a duty of representation and starts wondering how he can do that as quickly and simply as possible.

Given Gary's biases, do you think he can fulfill his professional duty? Can Samantha receive justice? What do you think Gary should do in this case?

9.6.3 A just allocation of health-care resources

County hospitals are very much at the mercy of the shifting winds of politics. Because they carry the largest burden for treating the medically indigent and, especially, undocumented immigrants, such hospitals are constantly on the hunt for ways to increase revenue and, through that, improve care.

When state or local coffers are full and when legislative bodies lean left, the hospitals generally do fine, either through generous – they would say "adequate" – reimbursement structures or by direct public grants. When money is tight and when the politics lean right, the hospitals are much more constrained in what they can do, in particular who they can treat and how intensively.

Some have resorted to a version of a mandatory co-payment. In order to be treated for anything other than an emergency, patients have to provide a nominal payment up front, typically $35 to $50. While it is not exorbitant, even that amount is enough to keep some people from seeking treatment. This results in delays and worsening illness, with the result that a number of them end up in the emergency room much sicker and in need of much more intensive treatment.

Still, hospitals have concluded that such co-payments are financially smart. Some of those who do not seek treatment get well on their own, the hospital gets at least a small amount from those who can pay, and the more serious cases that make it to the emergency room will likely have the bulk of their treatment covered by required state and federal reimbursements.

No one thinks that this is a rationally sound policy. In the long run it is far more expensive, not just in the more intensive treatment that is required in cases that delay seeking treatment, but also in lost wages and the spread of illnesses. But attempts to come up with different models have historically run into the buzz saw of politics. Insurance companies, physician and hospital groups, drug companies, medical equipment manufacturers, and malpractice attorneys all jump into the fray demanding that their sector not be the one to take a hit. Add to this the politics of poverty and of immigration, and you can see just how incredibly difficult it is to come up with just health-care finance policies.

If you were king or queen of the world and also committed to using the best possible principles of distributive justice, how would you design, at least in broad outline, an ethically sound health-care finance system?

NOTES

1. I am the hospital's consulting ethicist and had several conversations with key members of their administration during this time.
2. A third component, retributive justice, is primarily concerned with questions of punishment and thus is not germane to our discussion here.
3. Chronic obstructive pulmonary disease is a debilitating disease, typically though not always of the lungs, which is related to cigarette smoking and is exacerbated by drug and alcohol abuse. It is the third leading cause of death in the United States.
4. Rare but not completely absent. As many of those who supported Donald Trump's presidential campaign made clear, explicit appeals to bigoted rhetoric (e.g., Trump's suggestion that all Muslims be prevented from entering the United States, along with his earlier disparagement of a disabled reporter and bigoted comments about Mexican immigrants being rapists and disease carriers) were not only tolerated but occasionally celebrated.

REFERENCES

Chiaramonte, Gabrielle R., and Friend, Ronald. 2006. "Medical Students' and Residents' Gender Bias in the Diagnosis, Treatment, and Interpretation of Coronary Heart Disease Symptoms." *Health Psychology* 25 (3): 255–266.

Dworkin, Ronald. 2013. *Justice for Hedgehogs.* Cambridge, MA: Belknap Press.

Hagedorn, Emily. 2007. "Couple: Hospital's Refusal of Visi was Discrimination." Bakersfield.com. http://www.bakersfield.com/news/2007/03/08/couple-hospital-s-refusal-of-visit-was-discrimination.html, accessed August 25, 2017.

Halloway, Kali. 2014. "Racism Is So Insidious, Even Black People Underestimate It." *Guardian*, September 29. http://www.theguardian.com/commentisfree/2014/sep/29/racism-black-people-experience, accessed August 25, 2017.

Malik, Sarah E., and Salerno, Jessica M. 2014. "Moral Outrage Drives Biases against Gay and Lesbian Individuals in Legal Judgments." Jury Expert. http://www.thejuryexpert.com/2014/11/moral-outrage-drives-biases-against-gay-and-lesbian-individuals-in-legal-judgments, accessed August 25, 2017.

Meyers, Christopher. 2015. "Journalistic Objectivity." In *International Encyclopedia of Ethics*, edited by Hugh Lafollette. Hoboken, NJ: John Wiley & Sons.

Mower, Deborah S. 2014. "Reflections on a Culture of Sensitivity." *Teaching Ethics* 15 (2): 227–244.

Nozick, Robert. 1974. *Anarchy, State and Utopia.* New York: Basic Books.

Okonofua, Jason A., and Eberhardt, Jennifer L. 2015. "Two Strikes: Race and the Disciplining of Young Students." *Psychological Science* 26 (5): 617–624.

Rawls, John. (1971) 1999. *A Theory of Justice*, rev. ed. Cambridge, MA: Belknap Press.

Sandel, Michael J. 1998. *Liberalism and the Limits of Justice*, 2nd ed. Cambridge: Cambridge University Press.

Walzer, Michael. 1984. *Spheres of Justice: A Defense of Pluralism and Equality.* New York: Basic Books.

Werhane, Patricia. 1999. *Moral Imagination and Management Decision Making.* New York: Oxford University Press.

Zimbardo, Philip. 2008. *The Lucifer Effect: Understanding How Good People Turn Evil.* New York: Random House.

Epilogue: Democratization and the Changing of Professions

Some History   184

Democratization   185

Transforming Society and the Professions   187

Notes   189

References   189

"I almost qualified."

The Professional Ethics Toolkit, First Edition. Christopher Meyers.
© 2018 John Wiley & Sons Ltd. Published 2018 by John Wiley & Sons Ltd.

Recall that at the outset of this book I noted that much of what was to follow was an idealization. That is often the goal of an ethics text, to set out what it would mean to live and work by the highest ethical standards, realizing that reaching the top – all the time and in all places – is no doubt unrealistic. Even Kant acknowledged that, because humans are not only rational, we will often make choices driven by heteronomous drives (e.g., external pressures, internal emotions, or sheer laziness). But knowing that we will not always be able to recognize and do the right thing hardly means that we should not *try* to do so; even failed attempts reveal us to be persons of character.

All this certainly applies to professionals. Even those who are most committed to the highest standards are, like the rest of us, also self-interested and tempted by the slew of enticements that make it harder to prioritize client well-being exclusively. You probably know one or more extraordinarily impressive professionals. They are no doubt fully trustworthy and consistently and reliably strive to do the right thing; that is, they are genuine role models.

But no doubt they also make ethical mistakes, sometimes from ignorance, sometimes from moral lapse, but as often as not from external factors that create obstacles that are too great to surmount. I hope this book has helped to reduce the likelihood of failings from ignorance, but there is not much a book can do about moral failing. By the time one has the intellectual, moral, and emotional maturity to read this, one's character is largely set and exhortations to virtue serve mainly as a reminder – a moral booster – that ethics should be foundational to one's self-identity.

This Epilogue, thus, focuses on the external, the coercive pressures and restrictive constraints that make doing the right thing so very tough. Was it ever different? Well, yes. Today's professionals are no less individually virtuous than their predecessors. In many ways, they are even better, particularly with regard to reduced bigotry and the associated commitment to treat all persons with equal dignity and respect.

But they also work in changed structural conditions. Some of those changes, those that genuinely transferred power to clients, have made a huge positive difference, particularly in terms of increased information dissemination and the associated promotion of autonomy. Other changes, however, have resulted in a *corporatizing* of the professions, with power shifting away from professionals but not toward clients. Instead, the power has gone to accountants and profit managers. Thus, rather than enhancing client autonomy, these changes have done the opposite: they have commodified professional–client interactions in a way that dehumanizes both, especially the client.

In this brief chapter I shall outline some of the history behind these changes and then discuss the challenges they present for achieving the best professional–client interactions and relationships. I will close with an appeal for a re-professionalization of the professions.

Some History

The 1960s and 1970s are best known for the countless ways in which power shifted. Exemplified in the old "Challenge Authority" bumper sticker, some of these shifts came about through violent confrontation, for example Civil Rights activism and protests against the Vietnam War. Other changes were rooted in the non-violence model celebrated by iconic leaders like Martin Luther King, Jr.

These movements changed history, rewriting discrimination law and disrupting long-held biases against women, African Americans, and other minorities. Although it took many more years, these early protests also laid the foundation for what has recently appeared to be a sudden transformation in gay and lesbian rights. While all of this took many years, the changes clearly resulted in major power shifts. Women are increasingly assuming positions of political and business authority and Hispanics/Latinos are an emerging political force that may fundamentally transform US politics in the coming decades. The changes led to the election of President Barack Obama in 2008, a prospect that was unthinkable even thirty years ago. The election of President Donald Trump in 2016, accompanied by campaign rhetoric that emboldened a racist underbelly in the United States, would seem to represent a return to pre-disruption times. However, I remain hopeful that it is but a temporary slowdown in what King called the "moral arc of the universe," with its tendency toward justice.[1]

Democratization

The various historical movements are sometimes categorized under the comprehensive notion of "democratization," given the consistent emphasis on a more egalitarian distribution of social, political, and economic power. They also directly impacted the professions, for both good and ill. Those who previously had a virtual power monopoly – white males – were the same group who almost exclusively populated the professions. For example, in 1970, nearly 90 percent of physicians were male and only 2 percent were African American (Silberger et al., 1987; Thernstrom and Thernstrom, 1998).

Shifting power and inclusivity

One of the goals of democratization was to make the professions more inclusive and there has clearly been progress. By 2012, over 48 percent of medical school graduates were female and women are expected to soon make up the majority of practicing physicians in at least seven disciplines.[2] And, while race progress has been slower, African Americans currently make up over 5 percent of practicing physicians (Thernstrom and Thernstrom, 1998). Even in the sciences there has been a significant gender shift: of all science doctorates awarded in 2012, nearly 50 percent went to women, with nearly 23 percent in the engineering fields.[3]

But democratization had another goal. Regardless of who the professionals were, they had to share power. The idealized version of that goal was to shift the power to clients, and this has substantially occurred. As we saw in earlier chapters, the old paternalistic model gave way, legally and culturally,[4] to one that insisted that clients be autonomous participants in important decision making.

Commercialization

Some of this transformation was direct and intended, a result of the era's general challenge to authority. But some was also a by-product of a commercialization of the provision of professional services. Although clients' power and choices have certainly increased, this has come alongside an even greater shift of power to corporations and government. One example is that technical and technological (including pharmaceutical) advances have occurred at such an astonishing rate that individual professionals are now heavily dependent on for-profit providers, for example drug representatives and software designers. This dependence has, in turn, increased the effective power of those providers, often at the expense of clients' well-being and professionals' autonomy.

What it means to be a professional in the early part of the twenty-first century has changed substantially from what it meant in the mid-twentieth century. Professions, and professionals, have become less autonomous, less effectively self-regulating, and much more businesslike and thereby more beholden to corporate and for-profit interests.

The following are some examples:

- Physicians increasingly practice under managed care contracts or as part of large groups where "productivity" is at least as important as quality of care. William May calls this the "Disneyfication" of the professions (May, 2001, 47), where the goal is to "get 'em in and get 'em out" as quickly as possible. In this environment, physicians are reimbursed for as few as eight minutes of the patient encounter. This means that patients often do not get the attention they need or, even more frequently, that doctors work ridiculously long hours, much of it technically unreimbursed.
- Even physicians who are hired as faculty members at university-affiliated hospitals are under growing pressure to create a profitable return from patient care. Further, these pressures come with a list of arcane billing procedures that eat up a huge chunk of their, or their assistants', time.

- Many of you reading this have never known a time when professionals did not advertise. Professional advertising is a relatively recent phenomenon, the result of a 1977 Supreme Court case (*Bates v. State Bar of Arizona*, 433 U.S. 350) which found the advertising ban imposed by Arizona State Bar to be unconstitutional with regard to free speech. Lawyers across the country quickly pounced on this new commercial freedom and other professions quickly followed suit. While it is not, of course, inherently unethical, advertising directly affects the professions' norms and motivations. Instead of being strictly a service for people in need, the profession necessarily becomes more businesslike. Add to this the astonishing availability of information via the Internet – which is not always accurate or relevant – and professionals increasingly complain of the loss of their professional status, of being turned into mere *agents* (May, 2001).

- Pharmaceutical companies have become among the most profitable and influential agents within health care, spending *billions* annually on prescription drug marketing. Patients thus come to their professionals armed – often quite weakly – with specific requests for products and services. This too often results in treatment choices that produce great returns for drug companies but are not necessarily in patients' best interest (Brody, 2005).

- Collegiate faculty are under relentless pressure to increase student–faculty ratios and to respond to external regulators, particularly accrediting bodies.

- Many professional groups have felt the need to unionize. Once anathema to the very idea of a profession, unions are now seen as a necessary response to the growing corporatization of their services.

——— Transforming Society and the Professions ———

This overview gives a sample of the range of ways in which democratization has transformed society generally and the professions specifically. The list focuses on the negative impacts, and they have been significant, particularly the various ways in which the professional–client relationship has become substantially instrumental, with all participants being increasingly viewed as mere agents or, worse, as the equivalent of transactional commodities.[5]

But democratization has also produced great benefits. For example, the power asymmetry between professionals and clients, while still common, is significantly lessened from its peak in the paternalistic era. As a result, it is far more likely that clients will be genuine partners in their professional encounters, achieving goals that more closely align with their autonomous life plans.

Further, as noted earlier, diversified access to professional roles has increased substantially, as has access to the associated educational opportunities. This entrée into key social institutions and related wealth opportunities helps reduce disparities between the social strata. And, in our increasingly information-driven economy, the Internet's democratization of data – when acquired and used intelligently – is a powerful equalizing force.

Democratization has thus shaped inherent tensions, creating both great potential for social improvement and a corrupting commodification of the professional–client encounter. The latter, if continued unchecked, will, I fear, be the ruin of the professions' core commitment to their normative foundations.

The solution, as always, is *balance*: enhancement of democratization's best features and reduction of its worst. Happily, a number of professions are directly addressing that balance by finding ways to re-emphasize traditional professional norms. For example, medical schools are stressing an ethics curriculum and engaging in professionalizing rituals like "white coat ceremonies," in which students beginning their medical education are "cloaked" while reciting the Hippocratic Oath.[6] Similarly, the American Bar Association is undertaking a number of social justice initiatives,[7] with such programs also set against the backdrop of publications pushing for a more professional cadre of lawyers (Kronman, 1995).

As I have stressed throughout this book, however, the ethical tone of professional practice will in large part come down to individuals. The professional who retains the normative core does so mainly because of her *character*. She sees what she does as a *calling*, not as a business or as just another way of earning a living. That is, she is a genuine professional.

NOTES

1. I write this just four weeks after the 2016 presidential election, with little to no evidence of how the Trump administration will continue or retard the progress to justice.
2. "Diversity in Graduate Medical Education; Women Majority in Seven Specialties in 2012." Medical Press. http://medicalxpress.com/news/2015-08-diversity-medical-women-majority-specialties.html, accessed August 25, 2017.
3. "Women, Minorities, and Persons with Disabilities in Science and Engineering." https://www.nsf.gov/statistics/2017/nsf17310/data.cfm, accessed August 25, 2017.
4. Compare, for example, media depictions of professionals from the 1960s with contemporary shows and movies. The earlier depictions generally presented professionals as the wise and empathetic sage, while today's are more likely to be philandering and self-interested chumps, bumbling their way through their professional and personal lives.
5. For a compelling analysis of how transactional relationships alter how we think of ourselves and those with whom we engage, see Halikias (2016).
6. "Arnold P. Gold Foundation White Coat Ceremony." http://www.medicine.uiowa.edu/osac/white_coat.html, accessed August 25, 2017.
7. "Other ABA Initiatives," American Bar Association. http://www.americanbar.org/advocacy/other_aba_initiatives.html, accessed September 2, 2017.

REFERENCES

Brody, Howard. 2005. "The Company We Keep: Why Physicians Should Refuse to See Pharmaceutical Representatives." *Annals of Family Medicine* 3 (1): 82–85.

Halikias, Dimitrios. 2016. "The Trouble with Incentives" (Review of *The Moral Economy: Why Good Incentives Are No Substitute for Good Citizens*, by Samuel Bowles). http://newramblerreview.com/book-reviews/economics/the-trouble-with-incentives, accessed August 25, 2017.

Kronman, Anthony. 1995. *The Lost Lawyer: Failing Ideals of the Legal Profession.* Cambridge, MA: Belknap Press.

May, William F. 2001. *Beleaguered Rulers: The Public Obligation of the Professional.* Louisville, KY: Westminster John Knox Press.

Silberger, A.B., Marder, W.D., and Willke, R.J. 1987. "Practice Characteristics of Male and Female Physicians." *Health Affairs* 6 (4): 104–109.

Thernstrom, Abigail, and Thernstrom, Stephan. 1998. "Black Progress: How Far We've Come, and How Far We Have to Go." Brookings. http://www.brookings.edu/research/articles/1998/03/spring-affirmativeaction-thernstrom, accessed August 25, 2017.

Index

abortion, 82
absolutism, 42–43
abuse of power, 22–24, 26
ACA *see* Affordable Care Act
accountability,
    and animals, 78
    and children, 78
    and morality, 44, 46, 57–58,
       63, 78–79
accountants, 23, 85
accreditation processes, 107–108
actions, 5–6
    and happiness, 49
    harmful, 41–42
    impact on future, 56
advertising, 155, 187
affinity relationships, 34–35
affirmative action programs, 175
Affordable Care Act (ACA,
    "Obamacare"), 99
African–Americans, 171,
    184, 185
age, 167
agency, 33

AMA *see* American Medical
    Association
amateurs, 15
American Bar Association
    (ABA), 188
American Medical Association
    (AMA), 20, 22, 25
animals, 51, 57
    accountability, 78
    dignity, 81
    punishment of, 88n3
    respect for, 81, 82
Annals of Internal Medicine, 5
apprenticeships, 17, 19, 25, 58
arbitrary factors, 163–164
architects,
    autonomy, 85
    evaluation of, 109
    and honesty, 156
architecture, 34
Aristotle, 58, 61
Arizona State Bar, 187
Armani, Frank, 123–124
artificial intelligence, 57, 88n4

The Professional Ethics Toolkit, First Edition. Christopher Meyers.
© 2018 John Wiley & Sons Ltd. Published 2018 by John Wiley & Sons Ltd.

arts, 32
assent, 76, 86, 96
assisted suicide, 81
athletes, 15
attorneys, 85, 114
  and client's confidentiality,
    123–124
  and conflict of interest, 127–128,
    141–142
  defense, 119, 138, 155
autonomy, 74–87
  characterization, 74–75
  of clients, 33, 96–97
  degrees of, 77, 80–83
  development, 81–82
  and freedom, 78
  and happiness, 79
  in health-care ethics, 69–70
  and life plans, 63
  Mill on, 79–80, 82
  parental, 100–101
  of professionals, 25, 74, 83
  and status, 78
  understandings of, 70–71

Bacon, Francis, 18
barbers, 36n3
Bates v. State Bar of Arizona, 187
Bayles, Michael, 23
beauticians, 15
Belge, Francis, 123–124
beneficence, 47, 53–54, 91
  and balance, 93–95
  and confidentiality, 122–123
  as "imperfect duty", 91
  moral standing, 92
  and parental autonomy, 101
  paternalistic, 95–97
Bentham, Jeremy, 49
betrayal, 117

bias, 170–171
  arbitrary, 135
  conflict of, 134–135
  detecting, 135
  gender, 171
  ideological, 60
  implicit, 170
  irrational, 135
  and just representation,
    178–179
  managing, 171–172
  and structural conflict, 138
bigotry, 163, 164, 165, 167
  covert, 170
  explicit, 170
blind obedience, 153
blood products, 77, 86
BMA see British Medical Association
body, 45
Bok, Sisela, 153–155
bribes, 132, 133
British Medical Association (BMA),
    20, 22, 25
Brown, Jerry, 101

California, 7–8, 26, 83, 172
  vaccinations in, 100–101
California Bar, 29
calling, 7, 22–23, 27, 189
categorical imperative, 42, 52
caveat emptor, 22, 155
Centers for Medicare and Medicaid
    Services (CMS), 107
Certified Public Accountant
    (CPA), 85
character, 131
  of professionals, 165
  promotion, 59
  strength of, 58
  virtuous, 149